Good Housekeeping

Smart Carb
Suppers

Good Housekeeping

Smart Carb
Suppers

Ellen Levine	**Editor in Chief**
Susan Westmoreland	**Food Director**
Susan Deborah Goldsmith	**Associate Food Director**
Delia Hammock	**Nutrition Director**
Sharon Franke	**Food Appliances Director**
Richard Eisenberg	**Special Projects Director**
Marilu Lopez	**Design Director**

Photography Credits
Brian Hagiwara: pages 5, 6, 15, 18, 27, 30, 33, 37, 49, 55, 64, 70, 115, 127, 141, 145, 152, 161, 163, 173, 178, 187, 189, 196, 204, and 207. Alan Richardson: pages 41, 83, 101, 106, 116, 120, 124, 166, 192, 195, and 199. James Baigrie: pages 8, 59, 73, 79, 81, 96, and 182. Mark Thomas: pages 13, 45, and 170. Rita Maas: page 137.

Book design by Liz Trovato

Library of Congress Cataloging-in-Publication Data Available

2   4   6   8   10   9   7   5   3

Published by Hearst Books
A Division of Sterling Publishing Co., Inc.
387 Park Avenue South, New York, NY 10016

Good Housekeeping and Hearst Books are
trademarks of Hearst Communications, Inc.

The Good Housekeeping Cookbook Seal guarantees that the recipes in this cookbook meet the strict standards of the Good Housekeeping Institute. Every recipe has been triple-tested for ease, reliability, and great taste.

www.goodhousekeeping.com

Distributed in Canada by Sterling Publishing
C/o Canadian Manda Group, 165 Dufferin Street
Toronto, Ontario, Canada M6K 3H6

Distributed in Australia by Capricorn Link (Australia) Pty. Ltd.
P.O. Box 704, Windsor, NSW 2756, Australia

Printed in China

ISBN 1-58816-437-3

Contents

Foreword   *7*

Introduction   *9*

Chicken and Turkey   *13*

Beef   *59*

Pork and Lamb   *101*

Seafood   *145*

Vegetables, Eggs, and Cheese   *187*

Index   *217*

Foreword

Welcome to *Good Housekeeping*'s collection of smart carbohydrate recipes.

If, like many people today, you want to cut back on the carbohydrates without giving them up, this book has recipes for you. All of these recipes, from Beef Burgundy to Grilled Tofu and Veggies, have a low amount of total carbohydrates—less than 25 grams per serving. Each has been triple-tested by the *Good Housekeeping* test kitchen to ensure fantastic results every time you make it.

Many of the entrees also have a side dish recipe on an adjacent page to help you prepare a whole menu that is low in total carbohydrates. In other cases we offer a simple suggestion of what you could serve with the main dish. Try the Pepper Crusted Filet Mignon with Garlic-Crumbed Tomatoes for a fancy family dinner. If you're hosting, try Honey-Glazed Spiral Cut Ham with our Creamy Mustard and Dill Sauce, and Collards with Pickled Red Onions. Want a simple one-dish meal for dinner? Thai Beef Salad, Orange Pork and Asparagus Stir-Fry, Curried Chicken with Mango and Cantaloupe Slaw, and Salad Niçoise are some of the fabulous one-dish smart carb meals included.

All of the recipes have their nutritional value listed at the end of each recipe, so you can mix and match sides with main meals to your liking. You'll soon discover that lowering the carbohydrate count does not mean sacrificing taste or limiting your foods. So treat yourself, family, and friends to some great smart carb recipes!

—Susan Westmoreland
Food Director, *Good Housekeeping*

Introduction

The message should be simple: Eat well to stay well. But what is eating well? Every diet expert seems to recommend something different. Most experts agree that it is not healthy to cut out an entire category of foods—such as carbohydrates—but instead recommend limiting the portion size.

Dietary Guidelines for Americans

The U.S. Department of Agriculture (USDA) recommends that everyone eat a wide variety of foods to get the calories, protein, vitamins, minerals, and fiber needed. In addition, the agency recommends that you:

- Control calorie intake to manage body weight.

- Be physically active every day.

- Increase daily intake of fruits and vegetables, whole grains, and nonfat or low-fat milk and milk products.

- Choose fats wisely for good health.

- Choose carbohydrates wisely for good health.

- Choose and prepare foods with little salt.

- Drink alcoholic beverages in moderation.

- Keep food safe to eat.

Nutrients: The Big Three

Our bodies need three essential nutrients: carbohydrates, proteins, and fats. Carbohydrates are the body's major source of energy, feeding the brain and nervous system. Complex carbohydrates (including starch and fiber) are long chains of sugar molecules, while simple carbohydrates are single sugar molecules, or two linked sugar molecules. Proteins are needed to help produce new body tissue. Fats store the energy the body needs, but too much of the wrong kind can lead to health problems, including cardiovascular disease. Saturated fats (found in meat, dairy products, coconut and palm oils) and trans fat (found in processed foods via partially hydrogenated oils) should be eaten sparingly, while monounsaturated fats (found in olive, peanut, and canola oils) and polyunsaturated fats (found mainly in safflower, sunflower, corn, soybean, and cotton seed oils and some fish) are healthier and should constitute the majority of the fat in your diet.

Carbohydrates

Grains form the base of the USDA's food guide pyramid, revised in 1996. They provide complex carbohydrates, vitamins, minerals, and fiber. The USDA recommends that these foods make up the bulk of your diet, and that you eat 6 to 11 servings of these foods each day. One serving equals 1 slice of bread, 1 ounce ready-to-eat cereal, or 1/2 cup cooked rice, pasta, or cereal. The generous recommendation of 6 to 11 servings may seem high, but it adds up quickly, which many people do not realize. A typical bowl of cereal or pasta could easily equal 2, 3, or even 4 servings! With the pyramid's grains on bottom and fat on top, many people are overeating carbohydrates, which can lead to weight gain. This has given carbohydrates a bad name recently, but overeating anything will lead to weight gain!

Don't let the pyramid's listing of breads, pastas, and cereals at the bottom fool you into thinking those are the only sources of carbohydrates. Vegetables, fruits, and even dairy products also contain carbohydrates. If you are keeping track of your carb grams, don't forget to include those from the other food groups.

Simple carbohydrates are called simple because they consist of either one or two linked sugar molecules, and are found in table sugar, fruits, vegetables, and dairy products. Complex carbohydrates are found in whole grain foods, fruits, vegetables, and legumes (dried beans and peas). The chains, small and long, are broken down into glucose molecules in the small intestine, which are then absorbed into your bloodstream. As your blood sugar level increases, the pancreas produces insulin, which helps the glucose enter the body cells for use. As the glucose is absorbed, and the amount of glucose in the bloodstream decrease, the insulin levels drop.

Traditionally, carbohydrates that were classified as complex carbohydrates—such as bread, pasta, and other starches—were considered to be "good," and simple carbohydrates or sugars—such as table sugar, candy, and honey—were thought of as "bad." However, the USDA has noted a difference between intrinsic sugars, those found naturally in foods, and extrinsic sugars, those that are added into foods during processing and preparation. Intrinsic sugars include many simple sugars, such as those found in milk, lactose, and fruits, fructose, as well as the complex carbohydrates in whole-grain products—which are considered smart carb choices now. Extrinsic sugars are found in many highly processed foods, from bottled sauces and packaged mixes to sodas, cookies, and candies. There is no difference in the structure of the sugar molecules, whether intrinsic or extrinsic, and therefore, no difference in how the body breaks them down. However, foods that have large amounts of extrinsic sugars are typically lower in nutritional value, and can add too many unneeded calories.

Fiber, also long chains of carbohydrate molecules, is not broken down by digestive enzymes in the small intestine, and slows the absorption of other carbohydrates into the bloodstream, helping you feel full for longer. Since fiber, found in leafy green vegetables, whole grains, oats, fruits, and nuts, among other foods, does not break down to glucose, it does not boost insulin levels. Instead it is slowly fermented in the large intestine. The full feeling provided by fiber can help keep hunger from returning quickly, helping stave off the urge to snack. It also aids the excretion process, and studies have shown it helps decrease the risk of heart disease and diabetes.

Your best sources of smart carbohydrates are fruits, vegetables, and whole grains. But remember, overeating any carbohydrates, or any food for that matter, will still load those calories in!

Smart Carb versus Low-Carb Diets

When you think of comfort foods and home-style cooking, high carb counts are usually not far behind. The recipes in this book help you to cut carbs, but not to eliminate them. After much discussion and controversy, researchers, doctors and nutritionists have begun to move from plans that severely restrict carb intake into a more balanced camp. Good-Carb, or Smart Carb, is now the new buzz-word.

Prolonging life and preventing disease are essential factors in the consideration of a diet plan. It is proven that excess pounds make people sluggish, lethargic, unmotivated, and generally hinders the course you need to take towards a long and healthy life. It is on this point that the plethora of diets out there are providing conflicting information about what is a "healthy" way to lose and maintain weight. The Atkins, Zone, high-protein diets, and other fad diets have proven that, if followed exactly, can promote weight loss, as long as it cuts calories.

Many experts do stop short of recommending the extremely high levels of protein suggested by eating plans like the Atkins' diet because these plans so drastically cut carbohydrates—the initial phase of the Atkins' diet limits carbohydrates to 20 grams a day—and may lead to overconsumption of fat. When carbohydrates are not supplied to the body, the body will break down muscle protein and turn it into glucose.

Carbohydrates are a necessary part of a healthy diet because they provide the body with the energy it needs for physical activity and glucose, the simplest carbohydrate, is essential fuel for the brain. Carbohydrates are the major source of fiber in the diet. Many foods naturally rich in carbohydrates are also good sources of essential vitamins and minerals. Now we also know that white flour products, which have stripped the grain of its bran and wheat germ, the fiber rich parts of a grain, are not the best choices. Whole-wheat products keep the bran and wheat germ in tact, leaving the end product with its naturally occurring fiber.

While we do need to include carbs in our diet, eating a meal high in carbohydrates raises the blood sugar level, which in turn raises the insulin level.

When your insulin level is high, carbohydrates are the main source of energy for the body. When your insulin levels are low, your body uses a mixture of stored carbohydrate and fat to supply the energy. A good diet will provide carbohydrates for your brain, help your body use stored fat as energy, and keep the muscle protein intact.

To help promote weight loss, carbohydrates should still be a part of your diet, but in a more limited manner. Watch your overall calorie count; many experts agree that the calories consumed versus the calories expended are the key to controlling weight. Choose carbohydrate sources that are high in fiber, such as vegetables, or other naturally occurring carbs, such as nonfat or low-fat dairy, fruits, and whole-grain products.

Smart carbohydrate choices, included in these recipes, are considered a healthy part of a balanced diet.

Smart Carb Suppers

This book has three different types of suppers—one dish, two dish, and three dish—grouped according to the main dish. Each "supper" is marked by the icon shown above; the recipes that follow the icon belong in one dinner. Some of the two-dish suppers have a main-dish recipe with a serving suggestion mentioned after the recipe, while other multiple dish suppers have one or two accompaniment dish recipes following the main recipe. Each recipe has the nutrition listed afterwards, so recipes and accompaniment dishes can be mixed and matched however you like.

Chicken and Turkey

Coq au Vin

PREP 1 hour 15 minutes   **BAKE** 40 minutes   **MAKES** 6 main-dish servings

Chicken in Red Wine is a French bistro classic that fits in well with a smart-carb lifestyle.

4	slices bacon, cut into 1/2-inch pieces	1	package (12 ounces) mushrooms, each cut in half or into quarters if large
4	pounds bone-in chicken parts (thighs, drumsticks, and/or breasts), skin removed	2	tablespoons butter or margarine
1/2	teaspoon salt	3	tablespoons all-purpose flour
1/4	teaspoon coarsely ground pepper	1 1/2	cups dry red wine
1	small onion, finely chopped	1	cup chicken broth
1	carrot, finely chopped	2	tablespoons tomato paste
1	celery stalk, finely chopped	2	bay leaves
20	pearl onions (about half 10-ounce package or generous 1 cup), soaked in warm water and peeled	1/2	cup loosely packed fresh parsley leaves and stems, chopped

1. Preheat oven to 325°F. In 5-quart Dutch oven, cook bacon over medium heat until browned. With slotted spoon, transfer bacon to paper towels to drain.

2. Sprinkle chicken with salt and pepper. To bacon fat in Dutch oven, add half of chicken and cook over medium-high heat until browned on all sides, 10 minutes. With slotted spoon, transfer chicken to large bowl. Repeat with remaining chicken.

3. To same Dutch oven, add chopped onion, carrot, and celery; cook, stirring occasionally, until vegetables are tender, 10 minutes. With slotted spoon, transfer to bowl with chicken. Add pearl onions and mushrooms to Dutch oven and cook, stirring occasionally, until browned, 8 minutes. Transfer to bowl with chicken.

4. In same Dutch oven, melt butter. Add flour and cook, stirring frequently, 2 minutes. With wire whisk, whisk in wine until smooth. Stir in broth and tomato paste. Heat to boiling, whisking frequently; boil 2 minutes.

5. Return chicken, vegetables, and three-fourths of bacon to Dutch oven. Add bay leaves; heat to boiling. Cover Dutch oven and bake until chicken loses its pink color throughout, 40 to 45 minutes, turning chicken once.

6. To serve, discard bay leaves. Skim and discard fat. Transfer Coq au Vin to large serving bowl; sprinkle with parsley and remaining bacon.

Each serving: About 330 calories, 36 g protein, 13 g carbohydrate, 14 g total fat (6 g saturated), 3 g fiber, 108 mg cholesterol, 573 mg sodium.

Turkey Cutlets, Indian Style

PREP 15 minutes **GRILL** 5 minutes **MAKES** 6 main-dish servings

2	large limes	1	teaspoon ground coriander
1/3	cup plain low-fat yogurt	1	teaspoon salt
1	tablespoon vegetable oil	1	garlic clove, crushed with
2	teaspoons minced peeled		garlic press
	fresh ginger	6	turkey cutlets (11/2 pounds)
1	teaspoon ground cumin		

1. Prepare charcoal fire or preheat gas grill for covered direct grilling over medium heat.

2. Meanwhile, from 1 lime, grate 1 teaspoon peel and squeeze 1 tablespoon juice. Cut remaining lime into wedges; reserve for squeezing juice over cooked cutlets. In large bowl, mix lime peel and juice with yogurt, oil, ginger, cumin, coriander, salt, and garlic until blended.

3. Just before grilling, add turkey cutlets to yogurt mixture in bowl, stirring to coat cutlets. (Do not let cutlets marinate in yogurt mixture more than 15 minutes; their texture will become mealy.)

4. Place cutlets on hot grill rack. Cover grill and grill cutlets until they just lose their pink color throughout, 4 to 5 minutes, turning once. Serve with lime wedges.

Each serving: About 160 calories, 29 g protein, 3 g carbohydrate, 3 g total fat (1 g saturated), 0 g fiber, 71 mg cholesterol, 450 mg sodium.

Summer Squash with Herbs

PREP 15 minutes **COOK** 15 minutes **MAKES** 6 accompaniment servings

Fresh mint, oregano, and lemon accent tender summer squash.

2 tablespoons olive oil
1 small onion, finely chopped
3 small zucchini (6 ounces each), cut lengthwise in half, then crosswise into 1/2-inch-thick pieces
3 small yellow summer squashes (6 ounces each), cut lengthwise in half, then crosswise into 1/2-inch-thick pieces
1 garlic clove, crushed with garlic press

1 teaspoon chopped fresh oregano
1/2 teaspoon salt
1/4 teaspoon coarsely ground black pepper
2 tablespoons chopped fresh mint
1 teaspoon grated fresh lemon peel

1. In nonstick 12-inch skillet, heat oil over medium heat until hot. Add onion and cook, stirring frequently, until onion is golden, 5 to 7 minutes.

2. Increase heat to medium-high. Add zucchini, yellow squash, garlic, oregano, salt, pepper, and 1 tablespoon mint; cook, stirring often until vegetables are tender and golden, 10 minutes.

3. Transfer vegetables to bowl and toss with lemon peel and remaining 1 tablespoon mint.

Each serving: About 75 calories, 2 g protein, 7 g carbohydrate, 5 g total fat (1 g saturated), 3 g fiber, 0 mg cholesterol, 200 mg sodium.

Chicken with Pears and Marsala

PREP 15 minutes   **COOK** 15 minutes   **MAKES** 4 main-dish servings

1	teaspoon vegetable oil	2	Bosc or Anjou pears, peeled,
4	small skinless, boneless		cored, and quartered
	chicken-breast halves	3/4	cup chicken broth
	(1 pound)	1/2	cup dry Marsala wine
1/4	teaspoon salt	1	tablespoon cornstarch
1/8	teaspoon ground black	2	teaspoons chopped fresh
	pepper		sage leaves

1. In nonstick 10-inch skillet, heat oil over medium-high heat until hot. Add chicken; sprinkle with salt and pepper. Cook until chicken loses its pink color throughout, 10 to 12 minutes, turning once. Transfer to plate; keep warm.

2. To skillet, add pears and cook until browned on all sides, 3 to 5 minutes. Meanwhile, in cup, with wire whisk, whisk broth, wine, cornstarch, and sage.

3. Carefully add broth mixture to skillet; boil 1 minute to thicken slightly. Return chicken with any juices to skillet; heat through.

Each serving: About 195 calories, 27 g protein, 12 g carbohydrate, 3 g total fat
(1 g saturated), 1 g fiber, 66 mg cholesterol, 410 mg sodium.

SERVING SUGGESTION
Steamed broccoli and brown rice.

Panko-Mustard Chicken

PREP 15 minutes **BAKE** 12 minutes **MAKES** 4 main-dish servings

1 medium shallot, minced	1/2 cup panko (Japanese-style
6 teaspoons butter or	bread crumbs) or plain dried
margarine	bread crumbs
2 tablespoons Dijon mustard	4 medium skinless, boneless
with seeds	chicken-breast halves (11/4
2 teaspoons chopped fresh	pounds)
tarragon	1/4 teaspoon salt

1. Preheat oven to 475°F.

2. In small microwave-safe bowl, place shallot and 2 teaspoons butter. Cook in microwave oven on High 1 minute to cook shallot slightly. Stir in mustard and tarragon.

3. In another small microwave-safe bowl, place remaining 4 teaspoons butter. Heat in microwave oven on High until melted, 15 to 20 seconds. Stir in panko until mixed.

4. Arrange chicken breasts in 151/2" by 101/2" jelly-roll pan; sprinkle with salt. Spread mustard mixture evenly over breasts; top with panko mixture, patting on gently. Bake in top third of oven until chicken loses its pink color throughout, 12 to 15 minutes.

Each serving: About 272 calories, 35 g protein, 7 g carbohydrate, 10 g total fat
(5 g saturated), 0 g fiber, 107 mg cholesterol, 383 mg sodium.

Sesame-Asparagus Stir-Fry

PREP 10 minutes   **COOK** 10 minutes   **MAKES** 4 accompaniment servings

A dash of Asian sesame oil gives this quick asparagus side special character.

1 tablespoon sesame seeds	1 large garlic clove, minced
1 tablespoon olive oil	2 teaspoons soy sauce
1 1/2 pounds asparagus, trimmed and cut into 1 1/2-inch pieces	1/2 teaspoon Asian sesame oil

1. In nonstick 12-inch skillet, toast sesame seeds over medium-high heat until fragrant and golden, about 4 minutes. Transfer to small bowl.

2. To same skillet, add olive oil and heat until hot. Add asparagus, garlic, and soy sauce, and cook, stirring, until asparagus is tender-crisp, 6 to 8 minutes. Toss with sesame oil and sprinkle with sesame seeds before serving.

Each serving: About 75 calories, 4 g protein, 3 g carbohydrate, 6 g total fat (1 g saturated), 2 g fiber, 0 mg cholesterol, 180 mg sodium.

Roast Chicken Béarnaise

PREP 15 minutes **ROAST** 1 hour **MAKES** 4 main-dish servings

The flavors of the classic béarnaise sauce—shallots, tarragon, wine, and butter—are featured in this easy roast chicken.

1 teaspoon salt	4 sprigs fresh tarragon plus 1 tablespoon chopped fresh tarragon leaves
1/2 teaspoon coarsely ground black pepper	
1 chicken (31/2 pounds), giblets and neck reserved for another use	1/4 cup dry white wine
	1 teaspoon tarragon vinegar or white wine vinegar
1 large lemon, cut in half	1 tablespoon butter or margarine
3 medium shallots	

1. Preheat oven to 450°F. Sprinkle 1/2 teaspoon salt and 1/4 teaspoon pepper inside chicken cavity. Squeeze juice from lemon into cavity, then place halves inside cavity. Coarsely chop 2 shallots; add to cavity with tarragon sprigs. With chicken breast side up, tuck wing tips under back of chicken. With string, tie legs together.

2. Place chicken, breast side up, on rack in medium roasting pan (14" by 10"). Sprinkle with remaining 1/2 teaspoon salt and 1/4 teaspoon pepper.

3. Roast chicken until temperature on meat thermometer inserted in thickest part of thigh, next to body, reaches 175° to 180°F and juices run clear when thigh is pierced with tip of knife, about 1 hour. With tongs, tilt chicken to allow juices from cavity to run into roasting pan. Place chicken on warm platter; let stand 10 minutes.

4. Meanwhile, remove rack from roasting pan. Skim and discard fat from drippings in pan. Finely chop remaining shallot. Add wine, vinegar, and chopped shallot to roasting pan; heat to boiling over high heat. Remove pan from heat; stir in butter and chopped tarragon. Serve chicken with sauce.

Each serving: About 376 calories, 40 g protein, 1 g carbohydrate, 22 g total fat (8 g saturated), 6 g fiber, 166 mg cholesterol, 724 mg sodium.

Creamy Asparagus Soup

PREP 10 minutes   **COOK** 25 minutes   **MAKES** 5¹/2 cups or 4 first-course servings

A classic to celebrate Spring!

1	tablespoon butter or margarine	¹/2	teaspoon salt
1	small onion, coarsely chopped	¹/8	teaspoon ground black pepper
1¹/2	pounds asparagus, trimmed and coarsely chopped	¹/4	cup heavy or whipping cream
1	can (14¹/2 ounces) chicken broth or vegetable broth		sliced green onions and steamed thin asparagus spears (optional)

1. In 4-quart saucepan, melt butter over medium heat. Add onion and cook, stirring often, until tender and lightly golden, 8 to 10 minutes. Add asparagus and cook, stirring occasionally, 5 minutes.

2. Add broth, salt, pepper, and *1 cup water*; heat to boiling over high heat. Reduce heat to low; cover and simmer until asparagus is very tender, 8 to 10 minutes. Remove saucepan from heat.

3. In blender at low speed, with center part of cover removed to allow steam to escape, blend asparagus mixture in small batches until very smooth. Pour blended soup into large bowl after each batch. (If you like, use hand blender, following manufacturer's directions, to puree mixture in saucepan until very smooth.)

4. Return blended soup to saucepan. Stir in cream and heat through. Spoon soup into 4 bowls; top with green onions and asparagus spears if you like.

Each serving: About 126 calories, 4 g protein, 5 g carbohydrate, 10 g total fat (6 g saturated), 2 g fiber, 29 mg cholesterol, 794 mg sodium.

After-Work Chicken Soup

PREP 15 minutes **COOK** 15 minutes **MAKES** 8 cups or 4 main-dish servings

You can whip up this homey chicken soup, made with leeks and tiny bow-tie pasta, in just minutes!

1 medium leek (8 ounces)	1 can (14^1/2 ounces) chicken broth
1 tablespoon olive oil	
2 medium carrots, each cut lengthwise in half, then crosswise into ^{1}/4-inch-thick slices	^{1}/2 cup small bow-tie pasta (2 ounces)
	^{1}/2 teaspoon salt
1 medium celery stalk, thinly sliced	^{1}/8 teaspoon ground black pepper
^{1}/4 teaspoon dried thyme	12 ounces skinless, boneless chicken-breast halves, cut crosswise into very thin slices
1 bay leaf	

1. Cut off root and leaf ends from leek. Discard any tough outer leaves. Cut leek lengthwise into ^{1}/4-inch-thick slices. Rinse leek in bowl of cold water, swishing to remove any sand. With hand, transfer leek to colander to drain. Repeat process, changing water several times until all sand is removed. Drain and set aside.

2. In 4-quart saucepan, heat oil over medium-high heat until hot. Add leek, carrots, celery, thyme, and bay leaf; cook until leek wilts and vegetables are tender-crisp, 5 to 7 minutes.

3. Add broth, pasta, salt, pepper, and *3 cups water*; heat to boiling over high heat. Reduce heat to medium-low; simmer, covered, until pasta is just cooked, 5 minutes. Increase heat to medium; add chicken pieces and cook, uncovered, until chicken loses its pink color throughout, 3 minutes. Discard bay leaf before serving.

Each serving: About 220 calories, 23 g protein, 17 g carbohydrate, 6 g total fat (1 g saturated), 2 g fiber, 63 mg cholesterol, 800 mg sodium.

Tomato, Smoked Chicken, and Mozzarella Salad

PREP 15 minutes   **MAKES** 4 main-dish servings

A refreshing dish you can prepare in no time.

4	medium tomatoes (1¹/₂ pounds)	4	tablespoons thinly sliced fresh basil leaves
8	ounces fresh mozzarella cheese	2	tablespoons extravirgin olive oil
1	whole bone-in smoked chicken breast (1 pound)	2	teaspoons red wine vinegar
2	tablespoons snipped fresh chives	¹/₄	teaspoon salt
		¹/₈	teaspoon coarsely ground black pepper

1. Thinly slice 3 tomatoes. On large platter, arrange overlapping slices of tomatoes in circle around edge of platter. Thinly slice half of mozzarella; cut each slice in half. Tuck sliced mozzarella here and there between tomato slices.

2. Cut remaining tomato and mozzarella into 1/2-inch chunks. Remove skin and bones from chicken and discard. Cut meat into 3/4-inch chunks.

3. In large bowl, toss chunks of tomato, mozzarella, and chicken with chives, 2 tablespoons basil, 1 tablespoon oil, 1 teaspoon vinegar, 1/8 teaspoon salt, and pinch pepper.

4. Arrange chicken mixture in center of platter. Drizzle tomato and mozzarella slices with remaining 1 tablespoon oil and 1 teaspoon vinegar; sprinkle with remaining 1/8 teaspoon salt and pinch pepper. Top with remaining 2 tablespoons basil.

Each serving: About 340 calories, 26 g protein, 16 g carbohydrate, 22 g total fat (10 g saturated), 2 g fiber, 87 mg cholesterol, 880 mg sodium.

Chinese Five-Spice Grilled Chicken

PREP 10 minutes plus marinating   **GRILL** 25 minutes   **MAKES** 4 main-dish servings

Lots of flavor (from just a few ingredients) makes this a cinch for outdoor or indoor grilling.

1/4 cup dry sherry	1 chicken (3 1/2 pounds), cut
1 tablespoon Asian sesame oil	into 8 pieces, skin removed
1 teaspoon Chinese five-spice	from all but wings if you like
powder	1/3 cup hoisin sauce
1/4 teaspoon ground red pepper	1 tablespoon soy sauce
(cayenne)	1 teaspoon sesame seeds

1. In large bowl, stir sherry, sesame oil, five-spice powder, and ground red pepper.

2. Add chicken to spice mixture, and toss until evenly coated. Cover bowl and let stand 15 minutes at room temperature, turning chicken occasionally.

3. Prepare charcoal fire or preheat gas grill for covered direct grilling over medium heat.

4. Place chicken on hot grill rack. Cover grill and grill chicken, turning pieces once, until juices run clear when chicken is pierced with tip of knife, and removing to platter as they are done, 20 to 25 minutes.

5. In small bowl, mix hoisin sauce and soy sauce. Brush hoisin-sauce mixture all over chicken and return to grill. Cook until glazed, 4 to 5 minutes longer, turning once. Place chicken on same platter; sprinkle with sesame seeds.

Each serving without skin: About 350 calories, 41 g protein, 10 g carbohydrate, 15 g total fat (4 g saturated), 0 g fiber, 121 mg cholesterol, 595 mg sodium.
Each serving with skin: About 582 calories, 41 g protein, 12 g carbohydrate, 39 g total fat (11 g saturated), 0 g fiber, 161 mg cholesterol, 621 mg sodium.

SERVING SUGGESTION
Cucumber and cherry-tomato salad with the dressing of your choice.

Spiced Grilled Turkey Breast

PREP 35 minutes plus brining **GRILL** 25 minutes **MAKES** 12-main dish servings

Turkey isn't just for the holiday table! This flavorful grilled breast will wow them at your next barbecue.

Brined Turkey
- 1/4 cup sugar
- 1/4 cup kosher salt
- 2 tablespoons cracked black pepper
- 2 tablespoons ground ginger
- 1 tablespoon ground cinnamon
- 1 skinless, boneless turkey breast (4 pounds), cut in half
- 4 garlic cloves, crushed with side of chef's knife

Honey Glaze
- 2 tablespoons honey
- 2 tablespoons Dijon mustard
- 1 chipotle chile in adobo*, minced
- 1 teaspoon balsamic vinegar

Peach Salsa
- 3 pounds ripe peaches, peeled, pitted, and cut into 1/2-inch cubes
- 1 green onion, finely chopped
- 2 tablespoons fresh lime juice
- 1 small hot red pepper such as cayenne, seeded and minced
- 1/2 teaspoon salt

1. Prepare Brined Turkey: In 2-quart saucepan, heat *1 cup water* with sugar, salt, pepper, ginger, and cinnamon to boiling over high heat. Reduce heat to low; simmer 2 minutes. Remove saucepan from heat; stir in *3 cups ice water*.

2. Place turkey breasts in large zip-tight plastic bag; add brine and garlic. Seal bag, pressing out excess air. Place bag in bowl and refrigerate 24 hours, turning over occasionally.

3. Prepare charcoal fire or preheat gas grill for covered direct grilling over medium heat.

4. While grill heats, prepare Honey Glaze: In small bowl, stir honey, mustard, chipotle chile, and vinegar until blended; set aside.

5. Remove turkey from bag; discard brine and garlic. With paper towels, pat turkey dry and brush off most of the peppercorns. With long-handled basting brush, oil grill rack. Place turkey on hot rack. Cover grill and grill turkey 20 minutes, turning once. Brush turkey with glaze and grill, brushing and turning frequently, until temperature on meat thermometer inserted into thickest part of breast reaches 165°F, 5 to 10 minutes longer, depending on thickness of breast. (Internal temperature will rise 5°F upon standing.) Place turkey on cutting board and let rest 10 minutes to set juices for easier slicing.

6. While turkey rests, prepare Peach Salsa: In medium bowl, stir peaches, green onion, lime juice, hot red pepper, and salt until mixed. Makes about 4 cups.

7. Serve turkey hot, or cover and refrigerate to serve cold. Arrange sliced turkey and salsa on platter.

Canned chipotle chiles are smoked jalapeño chiles packed in a thick vinegary sauce called adobo. Look for chipotle chiles in Hispanic markets and in some supermarkets.

Each serving turkey: About 170 calories, 34 g protein, 4 g carbohydrate, 1 g total fat
(0 g saturated), 0 g fiber, 94 mg cholesterol, 555 mg sodium.
Each 1/4 cup salsa: About 30 calories, 1 g protein, 7 g carbohydrate, 0 g total fat,
1 g fiber, 0 mg cholesterol, 75 mg sodium.

If boneless turkey breast is unavailable, you will need to buy a 7- to 8-pound bone-in turkey breast and have the butcher bone, skin, and split it.

Watermelon Salad

PREP 10 minutes   **MAKES** about 8 cups or 12 accompaniment servings

6   cups (1-inch cubes) seedless
    watermelon (from 3³/4-
    pound piece)
3   Kirby (pickling) cucumbers
    (4 ounces each), unpeeled
    and thinly sliced

1   jalapeño chile, seeded and
    minced
3   tablespoons red wine vinegar
1/2 teaspoon salt

In large bowl, with rubber spatula, gently stir watermelon, cucumbers, jalapeño, vinegar, and salt. If not serving right away, cover and refrigerate up to 2 hours.

Each serving: About 30 calories, 1 g protein, 7 g carbohydrate, 0 g total fat, 1 g fiber, 0 mg cholesterol, 100 mg sodium.

Curried Chicken with Mango and Cantaloupe Slaw

PREP 25 minutes plus marinating   **GRILL** 10 minutes   **MAKES** 4 main-dish servings

A sprightly mango and cantaloupe slaw makes a great addition to curried chicken.

1   to 2 limes
1   container (6 ounces) plain low-fat yogurt
3/4   teaspoon curry powder
4   tablespoons chopped crystallized ginger
1   teaspoon salt
1/4   teaspoon crushed red pepper
4   medium skinless, boneless chicken-breast halves (11/4 pounds)

1/2   small cantaloupe, rind removed, cut into 2" by 1/4" matchstick strips (2 cups)
1   large mango, peeled and cut into 2" by 1/4" matchstick strips (2 cups)
1/2   cup loosely packed fresh cilantro leaves, chopped
1   head Boston lettuce lime wedges (optional)

1. From limes, grate 1/2 teaspoon peel and squeeze 2 tablespoons juice. In large bowl, with wire whisk, whisk 1 tablespoon lime juice and 1/4 teaspoon lime peel with yogurt, curry powder, 2 tablespoons ginger, 3/4 teaspoon salt, and 1/8 teaspoon crushed red pepper. Add chicken, turning to coat with marinade. Cover and let stand 15 minutes at room temperature or 30 minutes in refrigerator, turning occasionally.

2. Meanwhile, prepare slaw: In medium bowl, with rubber spatula, gently stir cantaloupe and mango with cilantro, remaining 2 tablespoons ginger, 1 tablespoon lime juice, 1/4 teaspoon lime peel, 1/4 teaspoon salt, and 1/8 teaspoon crushed red pepper; set aside. Makes about 4 cups.

3. Prepare charcoal fire or preheat gas grill for covered direct grilling over medium heat.

4. Grease grill rack. Remove chicken from marinade; discard marinade. Place chicken on hot rack. Cover grill and grill until chicken loses its pink color throughout, 10 to 12 minutes, turning once. Transfer chicken to cutting board; cool slightly until easy to handle, then cut into long thin slices.

5. To serve, arrange lettuce leaves on four dinner plates; top with chicken and slaw. Serve with lime wedges if you like.

Each serving chicken with lettuce: About 205 calories, 34 g protein, 5 g carbohydrate, 4 g total fat (1 g saturated), 1 g fiber, 92 mg cholesterol, 330 mg sodium.
Each 1/2 cup slaw: About 50 calories, 1 g protein, 13 g carbohydrate, 0 g total fat, 1 g fiber, 0 mg cholesterol, 150 mg sodium.

Beer Can Chicken

PREP 15 minutes   **GRILL** 1 hour to 1 hour 15 minutes   **MAKES** 8 main-dish servings

3 tablespoons paprika	1 teaspoon ground red pepper (cayenne)
1 tablespoon sugar	
1 tablespoon salt	2 chickens (3 1/2 pounds each), giblets and necks reserved for another use
2 teaspoons coarsely ground black pepper	
1 teaspoon onion powder	2 cans (12 ounces each) beer
1 teaspoon garlic powder	

1. Prepare charcoal fire for covered indirect grilling with drip pan as manufacturer directs*, or preheat gas grill for covered indirect grilling over medium heat.

2. In small bowl, combine paprika, sugar, salt, black pepper, onion powder, garlic powder, and ground red pepper.

3. If you like, rinse chickens with cold running water and drain well; pat dry with paper towels. Sprinkle 1 tablespoon spice mixture inside cavity of each chicken. Rub remaining spice mixture over chickens.

4. Wipe beer cans clean. Open beer cans; pour off 1/2 cup beer from each can and reserve for another use. With can opener (church key), make 4 more holes in top of each can.

5. With partially filled beer can on flat surface, hold 1 chicken upright, with opening of body cavity down, and slide chicken over top of beer can so can fits inside cavity. Repeat with remaining chicken and can. With large spatula, transfer chickens, one at a time, to center of hot grill rack, keeping cans upright. (If using charcoal, place chickens over drip pan.) Spread out legs to balance chickens on rack.

6. Cover grill and grill chickens until temperature on meat thermometer inserted in thickest part of thigh, next to body, reaches 175° to 180°F and juices run clear when thigh is pierced with tip of knife, 1 hour to 1 hour 15 minutes.

7. With tongs and barbecue mitts, remove chickens and cans from grill, being careful not to spill beer. Let chicken stand 10 minutes before lifting from cans. Transfer chicken to platter or carving board; discard beer.

If using a charcoal grill, you will need to add 10 fresh charcoal briquettes per side if more than 1 hour of cooking is required.

Each serving: About 350 calories, 39 g protein, 4 g carbohydrate, 19 g total fat (5 g saturated), 1 g fiber, 152 mg cholesterol, 985 mg sodium.

Ginger-Jalapeño Slaw

PREP 20 minutes plus chilling   **MAKES** about 8 cups or 8 accompaniment servings

Red and green cabbage costar in this Asian-accented slaw.

1/3   cup seasoned rice vinegar
2   tablespoons olive oil
2   teaspoons grated, peeled fresh ginger
1/2   teaspoon salt
2   jalapeño chiles, seeded and minced
1   pound green cabbage, thinly sliced (6 cups)

1/2   pound red cabbage, thinly sliced (3 cups)
3   medium carrots, finely shredded (1 1/2 cups)
2   green onions, thinly sliced
1   cup thinly sliced kale

1. In large bowl, with wire whisk, whisk vinegar, oil, ginger, salt, and jalapeños until blended. Add green cabbage, red cabbage, carrots, green onions, and kale; toss well to coat with dressing.

2. Cover and refrigerate coleslaw 1 hour before serving to allow flavors to blend.

Each serving: About 80 calories, 2 g protein, 12 g carbohydrate, 4 g total fat (1 g saturated), 3 g fiber, 0 mg cholesterol, 480 mg sodium.

Grilled Chicken with Red-Pepper Salsa

PREP 20 minutes **COOK** 15 minutes **MAKES** 4 main-dish servings

An easy salsa of roasted red peppers and olives adds zest to basic pan-grilled chicken breasts. Try the salsa with other favorite grilled meats and vegetables—and on sandwiches too.

Pan-Grilled Chicken
- 4 medium skinless, boneless chicken-breast halves (1¹/₄ pounds)
- ¹/₄ teaspoon salt
- ¹/₈ teaspoon ground black pepper

Red-Pepper Salsa
- 1 cup drained, jarred roasted red peppers (6 ounces), chopped
- 2 medium celery stalks, cut into ¹/₄-inch pieces
- ¹/₄ cup pimiento-stuffed olives, chopped
- ¹/₄ cup minced red onion
- 1 whole pickled jalapeño chile or pepperoncini, stem discarded, minced
- 1 tablespoon fresh lemon juice
- ¹/₂ teaspoon sugar
- ¹/₄ teaspoon salt
- lemon wedges (optional)

1. Prepare Pan-Grilled Chicken: Lightly grease grill pan; heat over medium heat until hot. Add chicken and sprinkle with salt and pepper; cook until chicken loses its pink color throughout, 12 to 15 minutes, turning once.

2. Meanwhile, prepare Red-Pepper Salsa: In small bowl, combine red peppers, celery, olives, onion, jalapeño, lemon juice, sugar, and salt. Stir until well blended. Makes about 2 cups salsa.

3. Cut chicken breasts into thick slices. Spoon salsa over chicken. Serve with lemon wedges if you like.

Each serving chicken with salsa: About 210 calories, 34 g protein, 6 g carbohydrate, 5 g total fat (1 g saturated), 1 g fiber, 91 mg cholesterol, 745 mg sodium.
Each ¹/₄ cup salsa: About 30 calories, 1 g protein, 6 g carbohydrate, 1 g total fat (0 g saturated), 1 g fiber, 0 mg cholesterol, 520 mg sodium.

SERVING SUGGESTION
Steamed green beans.

Orange and Sage Roasted Turkey and Gravy

PREP 45 minutes   **ROAST** 3 hours 45 minutes   **MAKES** 14 main-dish servings

Instead of a traditional stuffing, we stuff this holiday bird with orange and sage to flavor the turkey from the inside out. Bake the Sausage and Herb Bread Stuffing in a separate dish alongside the turkey.

1 fresh or frozen (thawed) turkey (14 pounds)	2 small onions, peeled and each cut into quarters
2 large oranges	2 cans (14 1/2 ounces each) chicken broth
1/2 cup loosely packed fresh sage leaves	1/4 cup all-purpose flour
1 teaspoon salt	
3/4 teaspoon coarsely ground pepper	

1. Preheat oven to 325°F. Remove giblets from turkey; set aside. Discard liver or save for another use. Cut neck into several large pieces.

2. With vegetable peeler, from 1 orange, remove 1 strip peel (4 1/2" by 3/4") and reserve for making gravy. Cut same orange into quarters. From remaining orange, grate 2 teaspoons peel. Reserve 3 whole large sage leaves for making gravy; finely chop 1/4 cup of remaining sage. In cup, mix grated orange peel, chopped sage, salt, and 1/2 teaspoon pepper.

3. Place orange quarters, onions, and remaining whole sage leaves inside body cavity of turkey. Fasten neck skin to back with 1 or 2 skewers. With turkey breast-side up, fold wings under back of turkey so they stay in place. If drumsticks are not held by band of skin or stuffing clamp, tie the legs together with string.

4. Place turkey, breast-side up, on small rack in large roasting pan (17" by 11 1/2"). Scatter giblets and neck pieces in pan around turkey. Rub turkey all over with chopped sage mixture. Cover turkey with a loose tent of foil. Roast turkey about 3 hours 45 minutes.

5. To brown turkey, remove foil during last 1$\frac{1}{4}$ hours of roasting time and baste with pan drippings occasionally if you like. Start checking for doneness during last hour of roasting. Turkey is done when temperature on meat thermometer inserted into thickest part of thigh next to bone but without touching bone reaches 175° to 180°F, and breast temperature reaches 165°F. (Internal temperature of turkey will rise 5° to 10°F upon standing.)

6. When turkey is done, place on large platter; cover with foil to keep warm. Prepare gravy: Remove rack from roasting pan. Strain pan drippings into 4-cup glass measuring cup or medium bowl, leaving giblets and neck in pan. Let drippings stand to allow fat to separate from meat juice.

7. Place roasting pan over medium-high heat, and cook giblets and neck until browned, about 2 minutes. Carefully add 1 can broth to hot roasting pan and heat to boiling, stirring until browned bits are loosened from bottom of pan; boil 3 minutes.

8. Spoon 2 tablespoons fat from drippings into 2-quart saucepan. Discard any remaining fat. Strain broth from roasting pan into glass measuring cup with meat juice. Discard giblets and neck. Add remaining can of broth and enough *water* to meat-juice mixture in cup to equal 4 cups total.

9. Stir flour into fat in saucepan; cook over medium heat, whisking constantly, until mixture turns golden brown, about 1 minute. Add meat-juice mixture, remaining 1/4 teaspoon pepper, and reserved orange peel and sage leaves. Cook over medium-high heat, stirring often, until gravy boils and thickens, 5 minutes. Discard orange peel and sage. Transfer to gravy boat. Makes about 4 cups.

10. To serve, pass gravy with turkey. Remove skin from turkey before eating if you like.

Each serving turkey without skin or gravy: About 245 calories, 48 g protein, 0 g carbohydrate, 4 g total fat (1 g saturated), 0 g fiber, 160 mg cholesterol, 235 mg sodium.
Each serving turkey with skin: About 390 calories, 52 g protein, 0 g carbohydrate, 18 g total fat (5 g saturated), 0 g fiber, 153 mg cholesterol, 250 mg sodium.
Each 1/4 cup gravy: About 35 calories, 1 g protein, 2 g carbohydrate, 2 g total fat (1 g saturated), 0 g fiber, 2 mg cholesterol, 250 mg sodium.

If using a frozen turkey, at least three days ahead, transfer from freezer to large tray and place in coldest part of refrigerator to thaw. Plan on 24 hours of thawing time for every five pounds.

Sausage and Herb Bread Stuffing

PREP 30 minutes   **TOAST/BAKE** about 1 hour   **MAKES** about 14 cups

1 1/2 loaves (16 ounces each) challah or other rich egg bread, cut into 3/4-inch cubes

1 package (10 ounces) fresh or frozen (thawed) pork-sausage meat

1/2 cup butter or margarine (1 stick), cut up

6 stalks celery, thinly sliced

1 jumbo onion (12 ounces), chopped

2 teaspoons salt

1 teaspoon coarsely ground pepper

1 cup loosely packed fresh parsley leaves, chopped

1 tablespoon fresh thyme leaves, chopped

1 tablespoon chopped fresh sage leaves

2 cans (14 1/2 ounces each) chicken broth

1 package (7 ounces) chopped mixed dried fruit (1 1/4 cups)

1. Preheat oven to 350°F. Divide bread between two 15 1/2" by 10 1/2" jelly-roll pans. Place pans on 2 oven racks and toast bread until golden, about 15 minutes, rotating pans between upper and lower racks halfway through toasting and stirring once. (If not completing stuffing now, cool toasted bread; store in plastic bag at room temperature up to 1 week.)

2. Meanwhile, heat nonstick 12-inch skillet over medium-high heat until hot. Add sausage and cook, breaking up sausage with side of spoon, until sausage is browned, 5 to 8 minutes. With slotted spoon, transfer sausage to very large bowl. Discard any fat remaining in skillet.

3. In same skillet, melt butter over medium heat. Add celery, onion, salt, and pepper, and cook, stirring occasionally, until vegetables are very soft, 20 minutes. Stir in parsley, thyme, and sage, and cook 2 minutes longer.

4. While vegetables are cooking, in 2-quart saucepan, heat broth and dried fruit to boiling over high heat. Remove saucepan from heat.

5. To bowl with sausage, add vegetable mixture, broth with dried fruit, and bread cubes; toss to mix well. Use to stuff 12- to 16-pound turkey. Or spoon stuffing into greased 13" by 9" baking dish or shallow 3 1/2-quart casserole. Cover with foil and bake in preheated 325°F oven 30 minutes. Remove cover; bake until heated through and lightly browned on top, about 15 minutes longer.

Each 1/2 cup: About 155 calories, 4 g protein, 18 g carbohydrate, 8 g total fat (2 g saturated), 2 g fiber, 20 mg cholesterol, 493 mg sodium.

Vietnamese-Style Chicken Salad

PREP 20 minutes plus standing   **GRILL** 10 minutes   **MAKES** 4 main-dish servings

Peanuts add a crunch to this scrumptious meal.

1/4 cup fresh lime juice (2 or 3 limes)

1 tablespoon sugar

1/4 teaspoon coarsely ground black pepper

4 tablespoons Asian fish sauce

1/2 small head green cabbage (12 ounces), cored and thinly sliced (5 cups)

2 medium carrots, cut into 2" by 1/4" matchstick strips

1 small onion, cut in half, then thinly sliced

4 medium skinless, boneless chicken-breast halves (11/4 pounds)

1 large bunch mint

1 large bunch cilantro

1/3 cup unsalted dry roasted peanuts, finely chopped

1. In large bowl, stir together lime juice, sugar, pepper, and 2 tablespoons fish sauce. Add cabbage, carrots, and onion, and stir until well combined. Let stand, covered, at room temperature up to 1 hour, or in refrigerator overnight to blend flavors.

2. Prepare charcoal fire or preheat gas grill for covered direct grilling over medium heat.

3. In large bowl, toss chicken with remaining 2 tablespoons fish sauce. Let stand at room temperature 15 minutes, turning chicken occasionally. Remove enough leaves from bunches of mint and cilantro to measure 1/2 cup each, loosely packed; chop. Reserve remaining mint and cilantro sprigs to garnish platter.

4. Place chicken on hot grill rack. Cover grill and grill until chicken loses its pink color throughout, 10 to 12 minutes, turning once. Set aside to cool.

5. When cool enough to handle, pull chicken meat into long thin strips. Add chicken, chopped mint, and cilantro to cabbage mixture.

6. To serve, stir half of peanuts into chicken salad. Arrange mint and cilantro sprigs on platter; top with salad and sprinkle with remaining peanuts.

Each serving: About 315 calories, 39 g protein, 18 g carbohydrate, 10 g total fat (2 g saturated), 5 g fiber, 90 mg cholesterol, 1,500 mg sodium.

Smart Carbs

Watercress and Peach Salad with Turkey

PREP 20 minutes plus standing   **MAKES** 4 main-dish servings

This makes a great summer meal.

2	to 3 limes
2	tablespoons honey
1/2	teaspoon Dijon mustard
2	tablespoons olive oil
1/2	teaspoon salt
1/4	teaspoon coarsely ground black pepper
4	ripe large peaches (2 pounds), peeled, pitted, and cut into wedges

2	bunches watercress (7 to 8 ounces each), tough stems discarded
1/2	pound sliced deli turkey or ham, cut crosswise into 1/4-inch strips

1. From limes, grate 1/2 teaspoon peel and squeeze 3 tablespoons juice.

2. In medium bowl, with wire whisk, mix 1/4 teaspoon lime peel and 2 tablespoons lime juice with honey, mustard, 1 tablespoon oil, 1/4 teaspoon salt, and 1/8 teaspoon pepper until blended. Gently stir in peaches; let stand 15 minutes.

3. Just before serving, in large bowl, toss watercress and turkey with remaining 1/4 teaspoon lime peel, 1 tablespoon lime juice, 1 tablespoon oil, 1/4 teaspoon salt, and 1/8 teaspoon pepper. Transfer watercress mixture to platter; top with peach mixture.

Each serving: About 235 calories, 20 g protein, 25 g carbohydrate, 7 g total fat (1 g saturated), 3 g fiber, 47 mg cholesterol, 360 mg sodium.

Turkey Kabobs with Garden Tomato Jam

PREP 30 minutes plus marinating   **GRILL** 10 minutes   **MAKES** 6 main-dish servings

Cut lean turkey breast into cubes, then marinate in a savory spice mixture. After grilling, serve with a quickly cooked combination of tomato and onion, sweetened with raisins and orange juice.

Turkey

- 1 large garlic clove, crushed with garlic press
- 1 tablespoon olive oil
- 1 1/2 teaspoons chili powder
- 3/4 teaspoon paprika
- 3/4 teaspoon salt
- 1/4 teaspoon ground red pepper (cayenne)
- 1/4 teaspoon ground black pepper
- 2 pounds skinless, boneless turkey breast, cut into 1 1/2-inch cubes

Tomato Jam

- 1 navel orange
- 1 tablespoon olive oil
- 1 small onion, chopped
- 1 pound plum tomatoes (7 large), seeded and cut into 1/4-inch cubes
- 1/3 cup golden raisins
- 1/4 teaspoon salt
- 1/4 cup loosely packed fresh cilantro leaves, chopped

1. Prepare Turkey: In large zip-tight plastic bag, combine garlic, oil, chili powder, paprika, salt, ground red pepper, and black pepper. Add turkey to bag, turning to coat with spice mixture. Seal bag, pressing out excess air. Place bag on plate; refrigerate at least 15 minutes or up to 1 hour.

2. Prepare charcoal grill or preheat gas grill for direct grilling over medium heat.

3. Meanwhile, prepare Tomato Jam: From orange, grate 1 teaspoon peel and squeeze 1/4 cup juice. In 10-inch skillet, heat oil over medium-low heat. Add onion and cook, stirring occasionally, until golden, about 5 minutes. Add tomatoes, raisins, salt, orange peel, and orange juice. Increase heat to medium-high; cook until tomatoes soften and liquid evaporates, about 6 minutes. Remove skillet from heat. Makes about 1 1/2 cups.

4. Thread turkey on 4 skewers. Place skewers on hot grill rack. Grill, turning occasionally, until turkey loses its pink color throughout, about 10 minutes. Stir chopped cilantro into Tomato Jam; serve with turkey.

Each serving turkey only: About 175 calories, 34 g protein, 1 g carbohydrate, 3 g total fat (1 g saturated), 0 g fiber, 94 mg cholesterol, 355 mg sodium.
Each 1/4 cup jam: About 75 calories, 1 g protein, 13 g carbohydrate, 3 g total fat (0 g saturated), 2 g fiber, 0 mg cholesterol, 105 mg sodium.

Arugula and Watercress Salad

4   teaspoons sherry vinegar or
    red wine vinegar
1/2 teaspoon Dijon mustard
    with seeds
1/8 teaspoon coarsely ground
    black pepper
3   tablespoons olive oil

1   bag (4 ounces) baby arugula
    (4 cups)
1   bag (4 ounces) watercress
    (4 cups)
1/4 cup toasted sliced almonds
    (one-sixth 7-ounce package)

1. In large salad bowl, with wire whisk, whisk together vinegar, mustard, and pepper. Add olive oil in thin, steady stream, whisking constantly, until dressing thickens slightly.

2. Just before serving, add arugula and watercress; toss to coat well. Sprinkle with almonds.

Each serving: About 95 calories, 2 g protein, 2 g carbohydrate, 9 g total fat
(1 g saturated), 1 g fiber, 0 mg cholesterol, 15 mg sodium.

Lemon-Fennel Roasted Chicken Pieces

PREP 20 minutes plus standing **ROAST** 25 minutes **MAKES** 4 main-dish servings

1 to 2 lemons
1 tablespoon olive oil
1 teaspoon salt
1/2 teaspoon coarsely ground black pepper
1/2 teaspoon fennel seeds, crushed
1 chicken (3 1/2 pounds), cut into 8 pieces and skin removed

1 large fennel bulb (1 1/2 pounds), trimmed and cut lengthwise into 8 wedges, or 1 celery heart, separated into stalks and cut into 3-inch pieces

1. From lemons, grate 1 teaspoon peel and squeeze ¼ cup juice. Preheat oven to 450°F.

2. In small bowl, combine lemon peel and juice with oil, salt, pepper, and fennel seeds. Arrange chicken and fresh fennel in large roasting pan (17" by 11 1/2"). Drizzle lemon-juice mixture over chicken and fennel; let stand 15 minutes.

3. Roast chicken and fennel, basting occasionally with pan juices, until temperature on meat thermometer inserted in thickest part of thigh, next to body, reaches 175° to 180°F, juices run clear when thigh is pierced with knife, and fennel is fork-tender, 25 to 30 minutes.

4. Transfer chicken and fennel to warm platter. Skim and discard fat from pan drippings. Spoon drippings over chicken to serve.

Each serving: About 280 calories, 34 g protein, 8 g carbohydrate, 12 g total fat (3 g saturated), 3 g fiber, 101 mg cholesterol, 725 mg sodium.

SERVING SUGGESTION
Steamed Brussels sprouts.

Thai Chicken Saté

PREP 45 minutes   **GRILL** about 5 minutes   **MAKES** 4 main-dish servings

Tender slices of skewered chicken are marinated in a curried coconut milk blend. Pickled cucumbers make a perfect partner.

12 (12-inch) bamboo skewers	1/4 cup creamy peanut butter
1 English (seedless) cucumber, thinly sliced crosswise	2 teaspoons soy sauce
1 1/2 teaspoons salt	1 teaspoon packed brown sugar
1 tablespoon Thai green curry paste	1/8 teaspoon ground red pepper (cayenne)
1/4 cup plus 1/3 cup well-stirred unsweetened coconut milk (not cream of coconut)	1/4 cup rice vinegar
	3 tablespoons granulated sugar
4 skinless, boneless chicken-breast halves (1 1/4 pounds), each cut diagonally into 6 strips	2 medium shallots, thinly sliced
	1 jalapeño chile, seeds and membrane discarded, minced

1. Place skewers in water to cover; let soak at least 30 minutes.

2. While skewers are soaking, in colander set over medium bowl, toss cucumber and salt; let stand 30 minutes at room temperature. In another medium bowl, stir curry paste and 1/4 cup coconut milk until combined. Add chicken and turn to coat. Let stand 15 minutes at room temperature, stirring occasionally.

3. Prepare charcoal fire or preheat gas grill for covered direct grilling over medium heat.

4. Meanwhile, prepare peanut sauce: In small bowl, with wire whisk, mix peanut butter, soy sauce, brown sugar, ground red pepper, remaining 1/3 cup coconut milk, and 1 tablespoon hot water until blended and smooth. Transfer sauce to serving bowl. Makes about 2/3 cup.

5. Drain cucumber, discarding liquid in bowl. Pat cucumber dry with paper towels. Return cucumber to bowl; stir in vinegar, granulated sugar, shallots, and jalapeño; refrigerate until ready to serve.

6. Thread 2 chicken strips on each skewer, accordion-style; discard marinade. Place skewers on hot grill rack. Cover grill, and grill until chicken loses its pink color throughout, 5 to 8 minutes, turning skewers over once.

7. Arrange skewers on platter. Serve with peanut sauce and pickled cucumbers.

Each serving without peanut sauce: About 260 calories, 34 g protein, 15 g carbohydrate, 6 g total fat (3 g saturated), 1 g fiber, 90 mg cholesterol, 525 mg sodium.
Each tablespoon peanut sauce: About 50 calories, 2 g protein, 2 g carbohydrate, 5 g total fat (2 g saturated), 1 g fiber, 0 mg cholesterol, 90 mg sodium.

Turkey Breast with Roasted Vegetable Gravy

PREP 40 minutes   **ROAST** about 2 hours   **MAKES** 8 main-dish servings

We slimmed down this Thanksgiving centerpiece by serving a turkey breast without its skin, degreasing the drippings, and thickening the gravy with roasted vegetables—but your guests will never know it's healthier!

1 fresh or frozen (thawed) bone-in turkey breast (6 pounds)	2 celery stalks, cut into 3-inch pieces
1/2 teaspoon salt	2 carrots, peeled and cut into 3-inch pieces
1/4 teaspoon ground black pepper	3 garlic cloves, peeled
2 medium onions, each cut into quarters	1/2 teaspoon dried thyme
	1 can (14 1/2 ounces) chicken broth

1. Preheat oven to 350°F. Place turkey breast, skin side up, on rack in medium roasting pan (14" by 10"). Rub turkey with salt and pepper.

2. Scatter onions, celery, carrots, garlic, and thyme around turkey in roasting pan. Cover turkey with a loose tent of foil. Roast turkey 1 hour. Remove foil and roast, until temperature on meat thermometer inserted into center of breast but not touching bone reaches 165°F, 1 hour to 1 hour and 15 minutes longer. (Internal temperature of turkey breast will rise 5° to 10°F upon standing.) When turkey is done, place on large platter; cover with foil to keep warm.

3. Meanwhile, prepare gravy: Remove rack from roasting pan. Pour vegetables and drippings into sieve set over 4-cup liquid measure or medium bowl; transfer solids to blender. Let drippings stand until fat separates from juices. Skim and discard fat.

4. Add broth to roasting pan. Stir until browned bits are loosened. Pour broth mixture through sieve into juices in measuring cup.

5. In blender at low speed, blend reserved solids with broth mixture and *1 cup water* until pureed. Pour pureed mixture into 2-quart saucepan; heat to boiling over high heat. Makes about 4 cups gravy.

6. To serve, remove skin from turkey. Serve sliced turkey with gravy.

Each serving turkey without skin: About 285 calories, 63 g protein, 0 g carbohydrate, 2 g total fat (1 g saturated), 0 g fiber, 174 mg cholesterol, 255 mg sodium.
Each 1/4 cup gravy: About 20 calories, 1 g protein, 3 g carbohydrate, 0 g total fat, 1 g fiber, 0 mg cholesterol, 125 mg sodium.

Arugula Salad with Citrus Vinaigrette

PREP 15 minutes   **MAKES** 8 accompaniment servings

1   jar (24 ounces) refrigerated red grapefruit or citrus segments (orange and grapefruit mix)
1   tablespoon cider vinegar
2   teaspoons Dijon mustard
1/2   teaspoon salt
2   tablespoons olive oil

2   bags (4 to 5 ounces each) baby arugula
2   medium celery stalks, thinly sliced
1   small yellow pepper, cut into 1/4-inch-wide strips
1/3   cup golden raisins

1. Drain juice from grapefruit segments into 2-cup liquid measuring cup. Pour 1/4 cup juice into small bowl; reserve remaining juice for another use. With wire whisk, mix in vinegar, mustard, and salt. In thin, steady stream, whisk in oil until vinaigrette is blended.

2. Place arugula on 8 salad plates. Sprinkle with celery, yellow pepper, and raisins. Top with citrus segments and drizzle with vinaigrette.

Each serving: About 90 calories, 2 g protein, 13 g carbohydrate, 4 g total fat (1 g saturated), 2 g fiber, 0 mg cholesterol, 175 mg sodium.

If you prefer your salad tossed, combine arugula, celery, pepper, and raisins. Just before serving, add vinaigrette and citrus segments and toss until coated.

Poached Chicken Piccata

PREP 10 minutes   **COOK** 12 minutes   **MAKES** 4 main-dish servings

Poaching keeps these chicken breasts moist and juicy. The flavorful poaching broth is used as the base for the piquant lemon-and-caper sauce.

1 **bay leaf**	2 **teaspoons cornstarch**
1/2 **teaspoon salt**	3 **tablespoons capers, drained**
4 **skinless, boneless chicken-breast halves (1 pound)**	2 **teaspoons butter or margarine (optional)**
1 **lemon, thinly sliced**	

1. In 10-inch skillet, heat *1 1/2 cups water* to boiling over high heat. Add bay leaf, salt, chicken, and 2 lemon slices; heat to boiling. Reduce heat to low; cover and simmer until chicken loses its pink color throughout, 10 to 12 minutes. With slotted spoon, transfer chicken to platter; keep warm.

2. Drain poaching liquid through coarse sieve set over medium bowl; discard solids. Return poaching liquid to skillet. In cup, mix cornstarch with *1 tablespoon water*. With wire whisk, beat cornstarch mixture into poaching liquid until blended; heat to boiling over high heat. Add capers; cook 1 minute, stirring constantly. Stir in butter if you like. Pour caper sauce over chicken and garnish with remaining lemon slices.

Each serving: About 154 calories, 27 g protein, 5 g carbohydrate, 4 g total fat (2 g saturated), 2 g fiber, 71 mg cholesterol, 574 mg sodium.

Lemon-Marinated Mushrooms

PREP 15 minutes plus standing   **MAKES** 6 accompaniment servings

The clean flavors of this simple dish go well with almost any menu.

1	pound small mushrooms, trimmed and cut into quarters	1	tablespoon plus 1 teaspoon fresh lemon juice
1/4	cup minced shallots	1/2	teaspoon salt
1/4	cup chopped fresh parsley	1/4	teaspoon ground black pepper
5	tablespoons olive oil		

In bowl, combine mushrooms, shallots, parsley, oil, lemon juice, salt, and pepper until mixed. Let stand at room temperature 1 hour, stirring occasionally. Serve, or refrigerate up to 6 hours.

Each serving: About 124 calories, 2 g protein, 5 g carbohydrate, 12 g total fat (2 g saturated), 1 g fiber, 0 mg cholesterol, 198 mg sodium.

Summer Squash and Chicken

PREP 15 minutes plus marinating **GRILL** 10 minutes **MAKES** 4 main-dish servings

1	lemon	4	medium yellow summer
1	tablespoon olive oil		squash and/or zucchini
1/2	teaspoon salt		(8 ounces each), each cut
1/4	teaspoon coarsely ground		lengthwise into 4 wedges
	black pepper	1/4	cup snipped fresh chives
4	skinless, boneless chicken		
	thighs (1 1/4 pounds)		

1. From lemon, grate 1 tablespoon peel and squeeze 3 tablespoons juice. In medium bowl, with wire whisk, whisk together lemon peel and juice, oil, salt, and pepper; transfer 2 tablespoons to cup.

2. Add chicken thighs to bowl with lemon-juice marinade; cover and let stand 15 minutes at room temperature or 30 minutes in the refrigerator.

3. Meanwhile, prepare charcoal fire or preheat gas grill for covered direct grilling over medium heat.

4. Discard chicken marinade. Place chicken and squash on hot grill rack. Cover grill and grill chicken and squash until chicken loses its pink color throughout and squash is tender and browned, 10 to 12 minutes, turning chicken and squash over once and removing pieces as they are done.

5. Transfer chicken and squash to cutting board. Cut chicken into 1-inch-wide strips; cut each squash wedge crosswise in half.

6. To serve, on large platter, toss squash with reserved lemon-juice marinade, then toss with chicken and sprinkle with chives.

Each serving: About 255 calories, 29 g protein, 8 g carbohydrate, 8 g total fat (3 g saturated), 3 g fiber, 101 mg cholesterol, 240 mg sodium.

Skillet Chicken Parmesan

PREP 10 minutes   **COOK** 10 minutes   **MAKES** 4 main-dish servings

Thinly sliced chicken sautéed in just a teaspoon of olive oil and part-skim mozzarella help lighten up this family favorite. Ready-made spaghetti sauce makes this a great weeknight recipe.

1	teaspoon olive oil	2	plum tomatoes, chopped
1	pound thin-sliced skinless, boneless chicken breast	2	tablespoons grated Parmesan cheese
1	container (15 ounces) refrigerated marinara sauce	1	cup loosely packed fresh basil leaves, sliced
4	ounces part-skim mozzarella cheese, shredded (1 cup)		

1. In nonstick 12-inch skillet, heat oil over medium-high heat until hot. Add half of chicken to skillet and cook, until chicken just loses its pink color throughout, about 4 minutes, turning once. Remove cooked chicken to plate; repeat with remaining chicken.

2. Reduce heat to medium. Return chicken to skillet; top with marinara sauce and mozzarella. Cover skillet and cook until sauce is heated through and mozzarella melts, 2 minutes. Sprinkle with tomatoes, Parmesan, and basil.

Each serving: About 295 calories, 36 g protein, 10 g carbohydrate, 11 g total fat (4 g saturated), 2 g fiber, 84 mg cholesterol, 660 mg sodium.

SERVING SUGGESTION
A cucumber and red onion salad.

Flame-Cooked Chicken Saltimbocca

PREP 10 minutes **GRILL** 5 minutes **MAKES** 8 main-dish servings

2 tablespoons fresh lemon juice	24 large fresh sage leaves
1 tablespoon olive oil	8 thin slices prosciutto (4 ounces)
8 skinless, boneless chicken-breast halves with tenderloins removed (2 pounds)	

1. Prepare charcoal fire or preheat gas grill for covered direct grilling over medium heat.

2. In large bowl, with fork, mix lemon juice and oil. Add chicken and toss to coat. Transfer chicken to waxed paper. Lay 3 sage leaves on each chicken breast. Wrap a slice of prosciutto around each breast; secure with toothpick if necessary.

3. Place chicken on hot grill rack. Cover and grill until chicken loses its pink color throughout, 5 to 7 minutes, turning chicken once.

Each serving: About 195 calories, 31 g protein, 1 g carbohydrate, 7 g total fat
(2 g saturated), 0 g fiber, 83 mg cholesterol, 410 mg sodium.

SERVING SUGGESTION
Tossed salad with choice of vinaigrette.

Beef

Beef Burgundy

PREP 1 hour   **BAKE** 1 hour 30 minutes to 2 hours   **MAKES** 10 main-dish servings

A hearty stew flavored with red wine, and a citrusy salad come together for a perfect midwinter supper.

2   slices bacon, cut into 1/2-inch pieces
3   pounds boneless beef chuck, trimmed and cut into 11/2-inch cubes
5   carrots, cut into 1/2-inch pieces
3   garlic cloves, crushed with side of chef's knife
1   large onion, cut into 1-inch pieces
2   tablespoons all-purpose flour
2   tablespoons tomato paste

1   teaspoon salt
1/2 teaspoon coarsely ground black pepper
2   cups dry red wine
4   sprigs fresh thyme
1   package (12 ounces) mushrooms, trimmed and each cut into quarters, or halves if small
1/2 cup loosely packed fresh parsley leaves, chopped

1. In 5- to 6-quart Dutch oven, cook bacon over medium heat until browned. With slotted spoon, transfer bacon to medium bowl.

2. Pat beef dry with paper towels. Add beef, in 3 batches, to bacon drippings and cook over medium-high heat until well browned on all sides, about 5 minutes. With slotted spoon, transfer beef to bowl with bacon.

3. Preheat oven to 325°F. To drippings in Dutch oven, add carrots, garlic, and onion, and cook, stirring occasionally, until vegetables are browned and tender, about 10 minutes. Stir in flour, tomato paste, salt, and pepper; cook, stirring, 2 minutes. Add wine and heat to boiling, stirring until browned bits are loosened from bottom of Dutch oven.

4. Return meat, meat juices, and bacon to Dutch oven. Add thyme and mushrooms; heat to boiling. Cover Dutch oven and bake until meat is fork-tender, 1 hour 30 minutes to 2 hours, stirring once. Skim and discard fat from liquid; discard thyme sprigs. Sprinkle with parsley to serve.

Each serving: About 295 calories, 36 g protein, 9 g carbohydrate, 11 g total fat (4 g saturated), 2 g fiber, 89 mg cholesterol, 375 mg sodium.

Vegetable Salad with Fresh Lemon Dressing

PREP 40 minutes   **MAKES** about 14 cups or 10 accompaniment servings

A pretty mélange of winter vegetables (fennel, celery, and carrots) is tossed with a piquant lemon dressing.

Lemon Dressing
- 2 large lemons
- 3 tablespoons olive oil
- 1 teaspoon salt
- 1 teaspoon sugar
- 1/4 teaspoon coarsely ground black pepper

Salad
- 1 large head Boston lettuce (12 ounces), leaves separated
- 6 small radishes, thinly sliced
- 3 celery stalks, thinly sliced diagonally
- 3 medium carrots, peeled and thinly shaved into wide strips with vegetable peeler
- 2 small fennel bulbs (10 ounces each), trimmed and thinly sliced
- 2 cups loosely packed fresh parsley leaves, coarsely chopped

1. Prepare Lemon Dressing: From lemons, grate 1 teaspoon peel and squeeze 3 tablespoons juice. In small bowl, with wire whisk, mix lemon peel and juice with oil, salt, sugar, and pepper. Cover and refrigerate if not serving salad right away.

2. Just before serving, line a large salad bowl with lettuce leaves. Coarsely chop remaining lettuce leaves. In another large bowl, toss dressing with chopped lettuce, radishes, celery, carrots, fennel, and parsley until vegetables are well coated; transfer to lettuce-lined bowl.

Each serving: About 65 calories, 1 g protein, 7 g carbohydrate, 4 g total fat (1 g saturated), 3 g fiber, 0 mg cholesterol, 275 mg sodium.

Grilled Steak Caesar Salad

PREP 25 minutes   **COOK** 10 minutes   **MAKES** 4 main-dish servings

This classic salad makes a tasty meal.

1/2   loaf French bread (4 ounces),
      cut into 3/4-inch cubes
      (3 cups)
5   tablespoons olive oil
4   anchovy fillets, drained
1   garlic clove, crushed with
      garlic press
1/4   cup grated Parmesan cheese
3   tablespoons fresh lemon
      juice (1 to 2 lemons)
1   teaspoon Worcestershire
      sauce

1/2   teaspoon dry mustard
1/2   teaspoon salt
1/4   teaspoon coarsely ground
      black pepper
2   boneless beef top loin
      (shell) steaks, 1 inch thick
      (8 ounces each)
2   medium heads romaine
      lettuce, cut crosswise into
      1/2-inch slices (10 cups)

1. Preheat oven to 350°F. In 15 1/2" by 10 1/2" jelly-roll pan, toss bread cubes with 1 tablespoon oil. Toast bread in oven, stirring occasionally, until golden brown, 15 to 20 minutes. Cool croutons in pan on wire rack.

2. Meanwhile, prepare dressing: In medium bowl, mash anchovies with garlic to form a paste. With wire whisk, mix in Parmesan, lemon juice, Worcestershire, mustard, 1/4 teaspoon salt, and 1/8 teaspoon pepper. Gradually whisk in remaining 4 tablespoons oil until well blended.

3. Preheat ridged grill pan over medium heat until very hot. Place steaks in pan; sprinkle with remaining 1/4 teaspoon salt and 1/8 teaspoon pepper. Cook steaks 5 to 6 minutes per side for medium-rare or until desired doneness. Transfer steaks to cutting board; let stand 10 minutes to set juices for easier slicing.

4. To serve, thinly slice steaks diagonally against the grain. In large serving bowl, toss romaine with steak slices, croutons, and dressing.

Each serving: About 465 calories, 32 g protein, 20 g carbohydrate, 29 g total fat (7 g saturated), 3 g fiber, 73 mg cholesterol, 785 mg sodium.

Pepper-Crusted Filet Mignon

PREP 15 minutes plus standing   **GRILL** 20 minutes   **MAKES** 4 main-dish servings

Time to fire up the barbecue: Grilled Sweet peppers are a nice foil to pepper-studded grilled steak.

1 tablespoon whole black peppercorns	3 medium peppers (red, yellow, and/or orange)
1 teaspoon whole fennel seeds	1 tablespoon minced fresh parsley leaves
4 beef tenderloin steaks (filet mignon), 1 inch thick (4 ounces each)	1 teaspoon olive oil
	3/4 teaspoon salt

1. Prepare charcoal fire or preheat gas grill for covered direct grilling over medium-high heat.

2. Meanwhile, on cutting board, with rolling pin, crush peppercorns and fennel seeds. With hands, pat spice mixture around edges of steaks. Cover and refrigerate steaks until ready to cook. (Can be prepared up to 24 hours ahead.)

3. Cut each pepper lengthwise in half; discard stems and seeds. With hand, flatten each pepper half.

4. Place peppers, skin side down, on hot grill rack. Cover grill and grill until skins are charred and blistered, 8 to 10 minutes. Transfer peppers to bowl; cover with plate and let steam at room temperature until cool enough to handle, 15 minutes. Reset grill temperature to medium.

5. Remove peppers from bowl. Peel off skins and discard. Cut peppers lengthwise into 1/4-inch-wide strips. Return peppers to same bowl and toss with parsley, oil, and 1/4 teaspoon salt.

6. Sprinkle steaks with remaining 1/2 teaspoon salt. Place steaks on hot grill rack. Cover grill and grill steaks 4 to 5 minutes per side for medium-rare or until desired doneness. Serve steaks topped with peppers.

Each serving: About 230 calories, 26 g protein, 9 g carbohydrate, 10 g total fat (3 g saturated), 2 g fiber, 71 mg cholesterol, 495 mg sodium.

Garlic-Crumbed Tomatoes

PREP 20 minutes   **ROAST** 15 minutes   **MAKES** 4 accompaniment servings

What could be simpler or yummier than this favorite summer side dish? When garden tomatoes are not at their peak, substitute fresh plum tomatoes, allowing one tomato per person.

2 tablespoons butter or margarine	1/4 cup grated Parmesan cheese
1 garlic clove, crushed with garlic press	1/4 teaspoon salt
1/2 cup fresh bread crumbs	1/8 teaspoon ground black pepper
1/4 cup loosely packed fresh parsley or basil leaves, chopped	2 ripe large tomatoes (12 ounces each), cored and cut crosswise in half

1. Arrange oven rack in upper third of oven. Preheat oven to 425°F. Line broiling pan or cookie sheet with foil.

2. In 10-inch skillet, melt butter over medium heat. Add garlic and cook, stirring, until fragrant, about 1 minute. Remove skillet from heat; stir in bread crumbs, parsley, Parmesan, salt, and pepper until mixed.

3. Place tomato halves, cut sides up, in prepared pan. Top tomatoes with crumb mixture. Roast until tomatoes are heated through and topping is golden, about 15 minutes.

Each serving: About 127 calories, 4 g protein, 11 g carbohydrate, 8 g total fat (5 g saturated), 2 g fiber, 20 mg cholesterol, 378 mg sodium.

Lighter Beef and Broccoli

PREP 25 minutes   **COOK** 12 minutes   **MAKES** 4 main-dish servings

A streamlined version of the popular Chinese dish—it's almost as quick as ordering takeout.

1	large bunch broccoli (1¹/₂ pounds)	¹/₄	teaspoon crushed red pepper
1	pound beef tenderloin steaks, trimmed, thinly cut into ¹/₈-inch-thick strips	1	teaspoon olive oil
		³/₄	cup chicken broth
3	garlic cloves, crushed with garlic press	3	tablespoons soy sauce
		1	tablespoon cornstarch
1	tablespoon grated, peeled fresh ginger	¹/₂	teaspoon Asian sesame oil

1. Cut broccoli flowerets into 1¹/₂-inch pieces. Peel broccoli stems and cut into ¹/₄-inch-thick diagonal slices.

2. In nonstick 12-inch skillet, heat *¹/₂ inch water* to boiling over medium-high heat. Add broccoli and cook, uncovered, until tender-crisp, 3 minutes. Drain broccoli and set aside. Wipe skillet dry.

3. In medium bowl, toss beef with garlic, ginger, and crushed red pepper. Add ¹/₂ teaspoon olive oil to skillet and heat over medium-high heat until hot but not smoking. Add half of beef mixture and cook, stirring quickly and frequently, until beef just loses its pink color throughout, 2 minutes. Transfer beef to plate. Repeat with remaining ¹/₂ teaspoon olive oil and beef mixture.

4. In cup, mix broth, soy sauce, cornstarch, and sesame oil until blended. Return cooked beef to skillet. Stir in cornstarch mixture; heat to boiling. Cook, stirring, until sauce thickens slightly, 1 minute. Add broccoli and toss to coat.

Each serving: About 245 calories, 28 g protein, 10 g carbohydrate, 11 g total fat (3 g saturated), 3 g fiber, 57 mg cholesterol, 1,010 mg sodium.

Thai Beef Salad

PREP 30 minutes plus marinating **GRILL** 10 minutes **MAKES** 4 main-dish servings

This hearty salad makes a great one-dish meal.

2	tablespoons Asian fish sauce	2	bunches watercress, tough stems discarded
2¹/2	teaspoons sugar		
1	beef top round steak, ³/4- inch thick (1 pound)	1	cup loosely packed fresh mint leaves
2	limes	1	cup loosely packed fresh cilantro leaves
3	tablespoons vegetable oil		
¹/4	teaspoon crushed red pepper	1	bunch radishes, each cut in half and thinly sliced
¹/4	teaspoon coarsely ground black pepper	¹/2	small red onion, thinly sliced

1. In 8- or 9-inch square baking dish, stir 1 tablespoon fish sauce and 1 teaspoon sugar. Add steak, turning to coat; marinate 15 minutes at room temperature or 1 hour in refrigerator, turning occasionally.

2. Prepare charcoal fire or preheat gas grill for covered direct grilling over medium heat.

3. Meanwhile, from limes, with vegetable peeler, remove peel in 2" by ³/4" strips. With sharp knife, cut enough peel crosswise into matchstick-thin strips to equal 1 tablespoon. Squeeze limes to equal 3 tablespoons juice. In small bowl, with wire whisk, whisk lime juice, oil, crushed red pepper, black pepper, and remaining 1 tablespoon fish sauce and 1¹/2 teaspoons sugar until blended.

4. In large bowl, toss lime peel, watercress, mint, cilantro, radishes, and onion; cover and refrigerate until ready to serve.

5. Remove steak from marinade. Discard marinade. Place steak on hot grill rack. Cover grill and grill steak 5 to 8 minutes per side for medium-rare or until desired doneness. Transfer steak to cutting board; let stand 10 minutes to set juices for easier slicing. Cut steak diagonally into thin strips.

6. Add steak and dressing to watercress mixture and toss until well coated.

Each serving: About 310 calories, 28 g protein, 7 g carbohydrate, 23 g total fat (4 g saturated), 2 g fiber, 73 mg cholesterol, 295 mg sodium.

Marinated Flank Steak with Grilled Summer Squash, Mushroom, and Feta "Lasagna"

PREP 30 minutes **COOK** 35 minutes **MAKES** 4 main-dish servings

The vegetable "lasagna" complements the steak in this delicious one-dish dinner. This recipe works well on an outdoor grill. Prepare gas or charcoal grill for direct grilling over medium-high heat. Grill as directed in recipe.

1   medium red pepper
2   tablespoons soy sauce
1   tablespoon minced fresh rosemary leaves
1   garlic clove, minced
5   tablespoons balsamic vinegar
4   tablespoons extravirgin olive oil
1   flank steak (1¹/₄ pounds)
2   small zucchini (6 ounces each)
1   small yellow summer squash (6 ounces)

1   large portobello mushroom (6 ounces), stem discarded
³/₄   teaspoon salt
³/₈   teaspoon ground black pepper
2   tablespoons minced fresh basil leaves
1   tablespoon minced fresh oregano leaves
2   ounces feta cheese, crumbled (about ¹/₂ cup)

1. Roast red pepper for relish: Heat large ridged grill pan over medium-high heat until hot. Cut pepper lengthwise in half; discard membrane and seeds. With hand, flatten each pepper half. Place pepper halves, skin-side down, in grill pan and cook until skin is charred and blistered, 3 to 4 minutes. Wrap pepper with foil; allow to steam at room temperature until cool enough to handle, 10 minutes.

2. Meanwhile, in large zip-tight plastic bag, mix soy sauce, rosemary, garlic, 3 tablespoons vinegar, and 1 tablespoon oil. Add steak to marinade, turning to coat both sides. Seal bag, pressing out excess air. Place bag on plate and refrigerate until ready to cook.

3. While steak is marinating, cut each zucchini and yellow squash lengthwise into 4 slices. Cut mushroom into ¹/₂-inch-thick slices. In large bowl,

toss vegetables with 1 tablespoon oil, 1/2 teaspoon salt, and 1/4 teaspoon black pepper; set aside.

4. Remove red pepper from foil. Peel off skin and discard. Cut pepper into 1/4-inch squares. In small bowl, mix red pepper with basil, oregano, remaining 2 tablespoons vinegar, 2 tablespoons oil, 1/4 teaspoon salt, and 1/8 teaspoon black pepper. Set relish aside. Makes about 1 cup.

5. Heat same grill pan over medium-high heat until hot. Add zucchini, yellow squash, and mushroom, in batches, and cook until lightly browned on both sides and tender, about 6 minutes, turning once. Remove vegetables to plate as they are done.

6. Remove steak from marinade; discard marinade. Pat steak dry with paper towels. In same hot grill pan over medium-high heat, cook steak 5 to 8 minutes per side for medium-rare or until desired doneness. Transfer steak to cutting board; let rest 10 minutes to set juices for easier slicing.

7. While steak is resting, assemble "lasagna": On each of 4 dinner plates, stack yellow squash, zucchini, and mushroom alternately with red-pepper relish and feta, ending with relish then feta.

8. To serve, thinly slice steak diagonally against the grain. Arrange steak slices on plates with "lasagna."

Each serving: About 430 calories, 33 g protein, 11 g carbohydrate, 28 g total fat (9 g saturated), 3 g fiber, 85 mg cholesterol, 810 mg sodium.

Skirt Steak with Chimichurri Sauce

PREP 15 minutes **GRILL** 6 minutes **MAKES** 4 main-dish servings

If you're lucky enough to have chimichurri sauce left over, try it as a sandwich spread. If made ahead, refrigerate sauce up to two days and bring to room temperature before serving.

Chimichurri Sauce
- 1 garlic clove, pressed
- 1/4 teaspoon salt
- 1 cup loosely packed fresh Italian parsley leaves, chopped
- 1 cup loosely packed fresh cilantro leaves, chopped
- 2 tablespoons olive oil
- 1 tablespoon red wine vinegar
- 1/4 teaspoon crushed red pepper

Steak
- 1 beef skirt steak or flank steak (11/4 pounds)
- 1/4 teaspoon salt
- 1/8 teaspoon coarsely ground black pepper

1. Prepare Chimichurri Sauce: In small bowl, stir garlic, salt, parsley, cilantro, oil, vinegar, and crushed red pepper until mixed. (Or, in mini food processor or blender, blend sauce ingredients until mixed.) Makes about 1/4 cup.

2. Prepare charcoal fire or preheat gas grill for covered direct grilling over medium heat.

3. Sprinkle steak with salt and pepper; place on hot grill rack. Cover grill and grill steak 3 minutes per side for medium-rare or until desired doneness.

4. Transfer steak to cutting board; let stand 10 minutes to set juices for easier slicing. Thinly slice steak crosswise against the grain. Serve with Chimichurri Sauce.

Each serving steak with 1 tablespoon sauce: About 300 calories, 40 g protein, 1 g carbohydrate, 14 g total fat (5 g saturated), 1 g fiber, 121 mg cholesterol, 380 mg sodium.

SERVING SUGGESTION
Grilled portobello mushrooms.

Beefsteak Florentine
with Autumn Tomato Salsa

PREP 25 minutes **COOK** 20 minutes **MAKES** 6 main-dish servings

Steak
- 1 tablespoon extravirgin olive oil
- 1 teaspoon salt
- 1 teaspoon coarsely ground black pepper
- 2 garlic cloves, crushed with press
- 1 beef loin porterhouse or T-bone steak, 2 inches thick (2 pounds)

Autumn Tomato Salsa
- 4 anchovy fillets, minced, or 1 teaspoon anchovy paste
- 1 medium shallot, thinly sliced
- 1/4 cup loosely packed fresh Italian parsley leaves, chopped
- 1 tablespoon extravirgin olive oil
- 1 tablespoon balsamic vinegar
- 1/4 teaspoon salt
- 1/4 teaspoon coarsely ground black pepper
- 1 pound ripe plum tomatoes (6 medium), cut into 1/2-inch pieces

1. Prepare Steak: In cup, mix oil, salt, pepper, and garlic. Rub mixture all over steak. Place steak on plate; let stand at room temperature 15 minutes.

2. Meanwhile, prepare Autumn Tomato Salsa: In bowl, mix anchovies, shallot, parsley, oil, vinegar, salt, and pepper. Add tomatoes; toss to coat. Set salsa aside. Makes about 2 1/2 cups.

3. Heat ridged grill pan over medium heat until very hot. Place steak in pan and cook 10 to 11 minutes per side for medium-rare or until desired doneness.

4. Transfer steak to cutting board; let stand 10 minutes to set juices for easier slicing. Slice steak and serve with tomato salsa.

Each serving steak: About 350 calories, 32 g protein, 1 g carbohydrate, 23 g total fat (9 g saturated), 0 g fiber, 82 mg cholesterol, 455 mg sodium.
Each 1/4 cup salsa: About 30 calories, 1 g protein, 3 g carbohydrate, 2 g total fat (0 g saturated), 1 g fiber, 1 mg cholesterol, 120 mg sodium.

Roasted Cauliflower with Red Pepper

PREP 15 minutes   **ROAST** 20 minutes   **MAKES** 6 accompaniment servings

1   medium head cauliflower
    (2 pounds), cut into 3/4-inch
    pieces
1   large red pepper, cut into
    1-inch pieces

1   garlic clove, finely chopped
1   tablespoon olive oil
1/2   teaspoon salt
1/4   teaspoon coarsely ground
    black pepper

Preheat oven to 450°F. In large bowl, toss cauliflower, red pepper, garlic, oil, salt, and pepper until evenly coated. Arrange vegetables in single layer in 15 1/2" by 10 1/2" jelly-roll pan. Roast vegetables until tender, about 20 minutes.

Each serving: About 45 calories, 2 g protein, 5 g carbohydrate, 2 g total fat
(0 g saturated), 2 g fiber, 0 mg cholesterol, 210 mg sodium.

Strip Steak with Red Pepper Vinaigrette

PREP 10 minutes   **COOK** 10 minutes   **MAKES** 4 main-dish servings

Red Pepper Vinaigrette
- 1 large garlic clove
- 1/4 cup loosely packed fresh parsley leaves
- 1 tablespoon fresh oregano leaves
- 1/2 cup red wine vinegar
- 1 teaspoon paprika
- 1 teaspoon chili powder
- 1/4 teaspoon salt
- 1/4 cup olive oil
- 1/2 small red pepper, cut into 1/4-inch cubes
- 1 plum tomato, seeded and chopped

Steaks
- 2 boneless beef top loin (strip) or rib-eye steaks, 3/4 inch thick (10 ounces each)
- 1/2 teaspoon salt
- 1/4 teaspoon coarsely ground black pepper

1. Prepare Red Pepper Vinaigrette: In blender, pulse garlic, parsley, and oregano until coarsely chopped. Add vinegar, paprika, chili powder, and salt, and blend until well combined. With blender running, add oil through hole in cover in slow, steady stream until mixture thickens. Transfer to small bowl; stir in red pepper and tomato. If not serving right away, cover and refrigerate up to 2 days. Makes about 1 cup.

2. Prepare Steaks: Heat nonstick 10-inch skillet over medium-high heat until very hot. Sprinkle steaks with salt and pepper. Place steaks in skillet; cook 3 to 5 minutes per side for medium-rare or until desired doneness. Serve with Red Pepper Vinaigrette.

Each serving steak: About 225 calories, 30 g protein, 0 g carbohydrate, 11 g total fat (4 g saturated), 0 g fiber, 82 mg cholesterol, 360 mg sodium.
Each tablespoon vinaigrette: About 35 calories, 0 g protein, 1 g carbohydrate, 4 g total fat (1 g saturated), 0 g fiber, 0 mg cholesterol, 40 mg sodium.

Okra with Tomatoes

PREP 20 minutes   **COOK** 35 minutes   **MAKES** 4 accompaniment servings

Okra and tomatoes are a classic combo in cuisines from India to the Mediterranean. Here's a favorite from the American South—okra braised with tomatoes, onion, and celery.

2 tablespoons olive oil	1 tablespoon chopped fresh
1 medium onion, chopped	parsley or 1 teaspoon
1 small green pepper, chopped	chopped fresh oregano
1 stalk celery with leaves,	1/2 teaspoon salt
chopped	1/4 teaspoon coarsely ground
2 garlic cloves, finely chopped	black pepper
1/2 cup water	12 ounces okra
1/2 teaspoon all-purpose flour	
1 can (141/2 ounces) diced	
tomatoes	

1. In 10-inch skillet, heat oil over medium heat. Add onion, green pepper, celery, and garlic; cook, stirring occasionally, until vegetables are tender, about 15 minutes.

2. In small cup, blend water and flour until smooth.

3. Stir tomatoes with their juice, parsley, salt, black pepper, and flour mixture into vegetables in skillet. Add okra and heat to boiling. Reduce heat; cover and simmer, stirring occasionally, until okra is tender, about 15 minutes.

Each serving: About 138 calories, 3 g protein, 17 g carbohydrate, 7 g total fat (1 g saturated), 6 g fiber, 0 mg cholesterol, 475 mg sodium.

London Broil with Garlic and Herbs

PREP 10 minutes plus marinating   **GRILL** 15 minutes   **MAKES** 6 main-dish servings

Round steak, not the most tender of cuts, benefits from a quick marinade of vinegar, garlic, and oregano.

2	tablespoons red wine vinegar	3/4	teaspoon salt
1	tablespoon olive oil	1/2	teaspoon ground black
2	garlic cloves, crushed with		pepper
	garlic press	1	beef top round steak, 1 inch
3/4	teaspoon dried oregano		thick (1 1/2 pounds)

1. Prepare charcoal fire or preheat gas grill for direct grilling over medium heat. In large zip-tight plastic bag, mix vinegar, oil, garlic, oregano, salt, and pepper. Add steak, turning to coat. Seal bag, pressing out excess air. Place bag on plate and marinate 15 minutes at room temperature.

2. Remove steak from marinade; discard marinade. Place steak on hot grill rack. Grill 7 to 8 minutes per side for medium-rare or until of desired doneness.

3. Transfer steak to platter. Let stand 10 minutes to set juices for easier slicing. To serve, thinly slice steak across the grain.

Each serving: About 200 calories, 26 g protein, 1 g carbohydrate, 10 g total fat
(3 g saturated), 0 g fiber, 72 mg cholesterol, 340 mg sodium.

Nectarine Salad with Prosciutto

PREP 10 minutes   **MAKES** 6 first-course servings

1 lime	6 thin slices prosciutto (4 ounces)
4 large nectarines (2 pounds), pitted and thinly sliced	1 bunch watercress (8 ounces), tough stems discarded
2 tablespoons olive oil	1 tablespoon coarsely chopped pistachios
1 teaspoon honey	
1/4 teaspoon salt	
1/8 teaspoon coarsely ground pepper	

1. From lime, grate 1/2 teaspoon peel and squeeze 2 tablespoons juice. In medium bowl, stir together lime juice and 1/4 teaspoon lime peel with nectarines, oil, honey, salt, and pepper until well combined. Let stand 10 minutes to blend flavors.

2. To serve, arrange prosciutto, nectarine mixture, and watercress on large platter; sprinkle with pistachios and remaining 1/4 teaspoon lime peel.

Each serving: About 160 calories, 7 g protein, 16 g carbohydrate, 9 g total fat (2 g saturated), 3 g fiber, 13 mg cholesterol, 570 mg sodium.

Korean-Style Sirloin

PREP 10 minutes plus marinating **COOK** 12 minutes **MAKES** 4 main-dish servings

1/2 cup reduced-sodium soy
   sauce
 2 tablespoons grated peeled
   fresh ginger
 1 tablespoon brown sugar
 1 tablespoon Asian sesame oil
1/4 teaspoon ground red pepper
   (cayenne)

 3 garlic cloves, finely chopped
 1 boneless beef top sirloin or
   top round steak, 1 inch thick
   (1 1/4 pounds)

1. In small bowl, stir together soy sauce, ginger, brown sugar, sesame oil, ground red pepper, and garlic.

2. Pour marinade into large zip-tight plastic bag; add steak, turning to coat. Seal bag, pressing out excess air. Place bag on plate; refrigerate 1 hour or up to 4 hours, turning bag over several times.

3. Heat ridged grill pan over medium-high heat until very hot. Remove steak from bag; pour marinade into 1-quart saucepan and reserve. Pat steak dry with paper towels. Cook steak 6 to 8 minutes per side for medium-rare or until desired doneness.

4. Transfer steak to cutting board; let stand 10 minutes to set juices for easier slicing. Meanwhile, add *2 tablespoons water* to marinade in saucepan; heat to boiling over high heat. Boil 2 minutes.

5. To serve, thinly slice steak diagonally against grain. Serve with cooked marinade.

Each serving: About 375 calories, 35 g protein, 9 g carbohydrate, 21 g total fat (8 g saturated), 0 g fiber, 102 mg cholesterol, 1,160 mg sodium.

SERVING SUGGESTION
Steamed broccoli with lemon and butter.

Lemony Veal and Baby Artichokes

PREP 30 minutes   **COOK** 25 minutes   **MAKES** 4 main-dish servings

Artichokes pair up perfectly with tender veal cutlets in this brothy sauce lightly flecked with tarragon. Once trimmed, baby artichokes are completely edible because the chokes haven't developed yet.

8 baby artichokes (12 ounces) or 2 medium artichokes	2 medium shallots, thinly sliced
salt	1 cup chicken broth
1 pound veal cutlets	1 tablespoon all-purpose flour
1 lemon	1 teaspoon minced fresh tarragon leaves
2 teaspoons olive oil	
1/4 teaspoon ground black pepper	

1. Trim baby artichokes*: Bend back outer green leaves and snap them off at base until remaining leaves are green on top and yellow at bottom. Cut off stem, level with bottom of artichoke. Cut off top half of each artichoke and discard.

2. In nonstick 12-inch skillet, heat *1/2 inch salted water* to boiling over medium-high heat. Add artichokes; reduce heat to medium-low and cook, covered, until artichokes are fork-tender, 12 minutes. Drain artichokes in colander; cool until easy to handle. Cut each baby artichoke lengthwise into quarters. Do not discard center portion.

3. Meanwhile, if veal cutlets are large, cut each crosswise in half. If necessary, with meat mallet, pound cutlets to even 1/8-inch thickness. From lemon, grate 2 teaspoons peel and squeeze 1 tablespoon juice.

4. In same skillet, heat 1 teaspoon oil over medium-high heat until hot but not smoking. Add half of cutlets; sprinkle with 1/4 teaspoon salt and 1/8 teaspoon pepper and cook until they just lose their pink color throughout, 2 minutes, turning once. Transfer cutlets to platter and keep warm. Repeat with remaining cutlets, 1 teaspoon oil, 1/4 teaspoon salt, and 1/8 teaspoon pepper (reduce heat to medium if cutlets are browning too quickly).

5. To same skillet, add shallots and *1/2 cup water* and cook over medium heat 1 minute. In cup, mix broth and flour. Increase heat to medium-high;

add broth mixture and lemon peel, and boil until slightly thickened, 1 minute. Add artichokes, tarragon, and lemon juice; cook 1 minute to heat through, stirring gently.

6. To serve, spoon artichokes with sauce over veal on platter.

If using medium artichokes, with serrated knife, cut 1 inch straight across top of each artichoke. Cut off stem; pull dark outer leaves from artichoke bottom. With kitchen shears, trim thorny tips off remaining leaves. Cut artichoke lengthwise into sixths. Scrape out choke, removing center petals and fuzzy center portion; discard. Repeat with remaining artichoke. Rinse artichokes well. Cook as in step 2.

Each serving: About 180 calories, 27 g protein, 7 g carbohydrate, 5 g total fat (1 g saturated), 2 g fiber, 89 mg cholesterol, 795 mg sodium.

Coffee-and-Spice Steak with Cool Salsa

PREP 30 minutes **GRILL** 15 minutes **MAKES** 6 main-dish servings

A dry rub of instant coffee, cinnamon, and allspice adds rich roasted, caramelized flavor to succulent flank steak. The crisp watermelon and cucumber salsa is a refreshing accompaniment to any meat.

Cool Salsa
- 1 lime
- 2 cups diced (1/4-inch) watermelon
- 1/2 English (seedless) cucumber, unpeeled and cut into 1/4-inch cubes
- 1 green onion, minced
- 1/4 teaspoon salt
- 1/8 teaspoon coarsely ground black pepper

Coffee-and-Spice Steak
- 2 teaspoons instant-coffee granules
- 1 teaspoon sugar
- 1 teaspoon salt
- 1 teaspoon coarsely ground black pepper
- 1/2 teaspoon ground cinnamon
- 1/4 teaspoon ground allspice
- 1 beef flank steak (1 1/2 pounds)
- 2 teaspoons olive oil

1. Prepare charcoal grill or preheat gas grill for direct grilling over medium heat.

2. Prepare Cool Salsa: From lime, grate 1 teaspoon peel and squeeze 2 tablespoons juice. In medium bowl, toss lime peel and juice with watermelon, cucumber, green onion, salt, and pepper. Cover and refrigerate salsa up to 2 hours if not serving right away. Makes about 3 1/2 cups.

3. Prepare Coffee-and-Spice Steak: In cup, mix coffee granules, sugar, salt, pepper, cinnamon, and allspice. Coat both sides of steak with oil, then rub with coffee mixture.

4. Place steak on hot grill rack. Grill steak 6 to 8 minutes per side for medium-rare or until desired doneness.

5. Transfer steak to cutting board; let stand 10 minutes to set juices for easier slicing. Thinly slice steak and serve with salsa.

Each serving steak: About 215 calories, 27 g protein, 1 g carbohydrate, 11 g total fat (4 g saturated), 0 g fiber, 47 mg cholesterol, 445 mg sodium.
Each 1/2 cup salsa: About 20 calories, 0 g protein, 4 g carbohydrate, 0 g total fat, 0 g fiber, 0 mg cholesterol, 80 mg sodium.

Baby Spinach and Beet Salad

PREP 20 minutes   **MAKES** 6 accompaniment servings

3   medium beets (1 pound
    without tops), peeled and cut
    into 2" by 1/4" matchstick strips
3   tablespoons seasoned rice
    vinegar
2   teaspoons soy sauce

1/2   teaspoon Asian sesame oil
1   bag (5 to 6 ounces) baby
    spinach
1   tablespoon sesame seeds,
    toasted

1. In medium bowl, stir uncooked beets, 1 tablespoon vinegar, 1 teaspoon soy sauce, and 1/4 teaspoon sesame oil. Let stand at room temperature 15 minutes or up to 2 hours to blend flavors.

2. Just before serving, in large salad bowl, toss spinach with remaining 2 tablespoons vinegar, 1 teaspoon soy sauce, and 1/4 teaspoon sesame oil. Top spinach with beets and their marinade; sprinkle with sesame seeds.

Each serving: About 60 calories, 2 g protein, 10 g carbohydrate, 1 g total fat
(0 g saturated), 4 g fiber, 0 mg cholesterol, 430 mg sodium.

Pan-Fried Steaks with Spinach and Tomatoes

PREP 15 minutes   **COOK** 15 minutes   **MAKES** 4 main-dish servings

Juicy top loin steaks infused with garlic and lemon are complemented by quickly sautéed vegetables.

1 large garlic clove, crushed with garlic press	1 teaspoon olive oil
1 teaspoon freshly grated lemon peel	1/2 cup chicken broth
1/2 teaspoon salt	1 teaspoon cornstarch
1/2 teaspoon coarsely ground black pepper	1 cup grape tomatoes or cherry tomatoes, each cut in half
2 boneless beef top loin or rib-eye steaks, 3/4 inch thick (10 ounces each), well trimmed	1 bag (10 ounces) prewashed spinach, tough stems discarded

1. In cup, with fork, blend garlic, lemon peel, salt, and pepper. Spread garlic mixture on both sides of steak.

2. In nonstick 12-inch skillet, heat oil over medium heat until hot. Add steaks and cook 5 to 6 minutes per side for medium-rare or until desired doneness. Transfer steaks to plate; keep warm.

3. In cup, mix broth with cornstarch. To same skillet, add broth mixture, tomatoes, and spinach. Heat to boiling over medium-high heat; cook, stirring, until spinach wilts, 1 to 2 minutes. Cut each steak in half; serve with spinach mixture.

Each serving: About 350 calories, 30 g protein, 3 g carbohydrate, 24 g total fat (9 g saturated), 6 g fiber, 92 mg cholesterol, 540 mg sodium.

Beef Tenderloins in Marmalade Pan Sauce

PREP 10 minutes   **COOK** 25 minutes   **MAKES** 4 main-dish servings

Filet mignon steaks are surrounded by a delicious pan sauce of caramelized onion and orange marmalade.

4 beef tenderloin steaks (filet mignon), 1 inch thick (4 ounces each)	1 garlic clove, crushed with garlic press
1/4 teaspoon coarsely ground black pepper	1/3 cup chicken broth
1/2 teaspoon salt	2 tablespoons orange marmalade
1 teaspoon olive oil	2 tablespoons balsamic vinegar
1 large onion, cut in half and thinly sliced	

1. Heat nonstick 12-inch skillet over medium-high heat until hot but not smoking. Add steaks; sprinkle with pepper and 1/4 teaspoon salt. Cook about 5 minutes per side for medium-rare or until of desired doneness (reduce heat to medium if steaks are browning too quickly). Transfer steaks to plate.

2. Heat oil in same skillet, over medium heat. Add onion and remaining 1/4 teaspoon salt. Cover and cook, stirring often, until tender and golden, about 10 minutes. Add garlic, broth, marmalade, and vinegar; heat to boiling. Cook, stirring, 1 minute. Return steaks and any juices to skillet; heat through, turning steaks to coat with sauce.

Each serving: About 235 calories, 24 g protein, 12 g carbohydrate, 9 g total fat (3 g saturated), 1 g fiber, 57 mg cholesterol, 440 mg sodium.

Black-Pepper Beef Roast with Shallot Sauce

PREP 25 minutes **ROAST** 1 hour 15 minutes **MAKES** 10 main-dish servings

Here's a terrific holiday dinner for busy cooks. The beans and tomatoes can be prepared ahead, and the no-fuss boneless roast just about cooks itself. Serve the roast with the shallot sauce made with pan drippings and a dollop of Horseradish Cream.

1 boneless beef rib-eye roast (3 pounds), tied
1 tablespoon plus 1 teaspoon cracked black pepper
1 tablespoon olive oil

1 teaspoon salt
1 medium shallot, minced (1/4 cup)
1 can (14 1/2 ounces) beef broth

1. Preheat oven to 350°F. Place beef on rack in medium roasting pan (14" by 10").

2. In small bowl, stir pepper, oil, and salt until blended. Rub pepper mixture on all sides of beef.

3. Roast beef until instant-read thermometer inserted into thickest part of beef reaches 135°F, 1 hour and 15 minutes. Internal temperature of meat will rise 5° to 10°F (medium-rare) upon standing. Or, roast to desired doneness. Transfer beef to large platter; let stand 10 minutes to set juices for easier slicing.

4. Meanwhile, prepare shallot sauce: Spoon 2 tablespoons fat from roasting pan into 10-inch skillet; discard any remaining fat. Cook shallot with fat in skillet over medium heat, stirring frequently, until tender and lightly browned, 3 to 5 minutes.

5. Add broth to drippings remaining in roasting pan; place pan over medium-high heat and cook, stirring to loosen brown bits, 2 minutes. Add broth mixture to skillet; increase heat to high, and heat to boiling. Boil until sauce is slightly reduced, 3 minutes. Pour into sauceboat and keep warm. Makes about 1 2/3 cups sauce.

6. To serve, remove string from beef. Cut beef into slices; serve with shallot sauce.

Each serving beef only: About 330 calories, 26 g protein, 1 g carbohydrate, 24 g total fat
(9 g saturated), 0 g fiber, 85 mg cholesterol, 300 mg sodium.
Each tablespoon sauce: About 10 calories, 0 g protein, 0 g carbohydrate, 1 g total fat
(1 g saturated), 0 g fiber, 1 mg cholesterol, 55 mg sodium.

Horseradish Cream

PREP 10 minutes plus chilling   **MAKES** about 13/4 cups

A simple condiment to serve with mouthwatering roast beef. Save some for sandwiches another day.

11/2 **cups sour cream**	1/4 **teaspoon coarsely ground**
1/4 **cup prepared white**	**black pepper**
horseradish	1/4 **cup snipped fresh chives**
1/4 **teaspoon salt**	

1. In small bowl, stir sour cream, horseradish, salt, and pepper until blended. Cover and refrigerate until chilled or up to 3 days.

2. To serve, stir in chives.

Each tablespoon: About 25 calories, 0 g protein, 1 g carbohydrate, 2 g total fat
(1 g saturated), 0 g fiber, 5 mg cholesterol, 30 mg sodium.

Green Beans with Oven-Roasted Tomatoes

PREP 30 minutes plus 3 hours roasting and cooling   **COOK** 15 minutes
MAKES 10 accompaniment servings

This dish is a real last-minute time-saver: Cook the green beans up to two days ahead, and roast the tomatoes up to one week ahead. If you're pressed for time, substitute jarred dried tomatoes packed in olive oil and herbs.

Oven-Roasted Tomatoes
- 2 pounds plum tomatoes (12 to 14 medium)
- 2 tablespoons olive oil
- 1/2 teaspoon dried basil
- 1/2 teaspoon dried thyme
- 1/2 teaspoon salt
- 1/8 teaspoon coarsely ground black pepper

Beans
- 1 1/2 teaspoons salt
- 2 1/2 pounds green beans, ends trimmed
- 2 tablespoons olive oil
- 1/4 teaspoon coarsely ground black pepper

1. Prepare Oven-Roasted Tomatoes: Preheat oven to 300°F. Line 15 1/2" by 10 1/2" jelly-roll pan with heavy-duty foil. Cut each tomato lengthwise in half. With spoon, scrape out seeds and discard. Place tomato halves in large bowl; toss with oil, basil, thyme, salt, and pepper. Place tomato halves, cut sides down, in jelly-roll pan.

2. Roast tomatoes until shriveled and partially dried, 3 hours. Cool tomatoes completely in pan on wire rack. If not using tomatoes right away, place in zip-tight plastic bag and refrigerate up to 1 week. (Recipe makes double the amount of tomatoes you will need for beans. Use remaining tomatoes in salads or sandwiches, or as a condiment.)

3. Prepare Beans: In 5- to 6-quart saucepot, heat *2 inches water* and 1 teaspoon salt to boiling over high heat. Add green beans; heat to boiling. Reduce heat to low; simmer, uncovered, until beans are tender-crisp, 5 to 10 minutes. Drain and rinse beans with cold running water to stop cooking; drain well. Refrigerate beans up to 2 days.

4. When ready to prepare dish, coarsely chop 1/2 cup roasted tomato halves; set aside. In 5- to 6-quart saucepot, heat oil over medium heat until hot. Add beans, pepper, and remaining 1/2 teaspoon salt; cook until beans are hot, about 5 minutes. Remove saucepot from heat; toss with chopped tomatoes.

**Each serving: About 80 calories, 2 g protein, 10 g carbohydrate, 5 g total fat
(1 g saturated), 4 g fiber, 0 mg cholesterol, 210 mg sodium.**

Steak with Shallot-Red Wine Sauce

PREP 5 minutes **COOK** 25 minutes **MAKE** 4 main-dish servings

1 teaspoon vegetable oil
2 boneless beef rib-eye steaks, 3/4 inch thick (12 ounces each)
1 teaspoon butter or margarine
1/2 teaspoon salt

1/4 teaspoon coarsely ground black pepper
2 medium shallots, finely chopped (1/4 cup)
1 cup dry red wine

1. In 12-inch skillet, heat oil over medium-high heat until very hot but not smoking.

2. Meanwhile, pat steaks dry with paper towels.

3. Add butter to skillet. Add steaks; sprinkle with salt and pepper and cook 4 to 5 minutes per side for medium-rare or until desired doneness. Transfer steaks to cutting board; keep warm.

4. To drippings in skillet, add shallots and cook over medium heat until browned and tender, 3 to 4 minutes. Add wine to skillet and heat to boiling over high heat. Boil 2 minutes.

5. To serve, thinly slice steaks and spoon wine sauce on top.

Each serving: About 531 calories, 30 g protein, 2 g carbohydrate, 40 g total fat (16 g saturated), 0 g fiber, 118 mg cholesterol, 397 mg sodium.

Escarole with Raisins and Pignoli

PREP 10 minutes **COOK** 20 minutes **MAKES** 4 accompaniment servings

Sweet raisins round out the flavor of slightly bitter escarole.

1	tablespoon olive oil	1/4	cup golden raisins
1	garlic clove, finely chopped	1/4	teaspoon salt
1	large head escarole (1 pound), coarsely chopped	2	tablespoons pine nuts (pignoli), toasted

In 5-quart Dutch oven, heat oil over medium heat. Stir in garlic and cook just until golden, about 30 seconds. Stir in escarole, raisins, and salt. Cover and cook 5 minutes. Remove cover and cook until escarole is tender and liquid has evaporated, about 10 minutes longer. Stir in pine nuts and remove from heat.

Each serving: About 101 calories, 3 g protein, 12 g carbohydrate, 6 g total fat (1 g saturated), 4 g fiber, 0 mg cholesterol, 169 mg sodium.

Tangerine Beef Stir-Fry

PREP 20 minutes   **COOK** 15 minutes   **MAKES** 4 main-dish servings

2	to 3 tangerines (1¹/2 pounds)	5	teaspoons vegetable oil
¹/4	cup dry sherry	1	bag (12 ounces) broccoli
2	tablespoons hoisin sauce		florets
2	tablespoons cornstarch	1	medium red pepper, thinly
2	tablespoons soy sauce		sliced
1	beef flank steak (1 pound), cut crosswise into ¹/8-inch-thick slices	1	tablespoon grated, peeled fresh ginger

1. From 1 tangerine, with vegetable peeler, remove peel. With small knife, remove any white pith from peel; slice peel very thinly and set aside. Squeeze ¹/2 cup juice from tangerines; stir in sherry and hoisin sauce and set aside. In medium bowl, combine cornstarch, soy sauce, and steak; set aside.

2. In nonstick 12-inch skillet, heat 1 teaspoon oil over medium-high heat until very hot. Add broccoli, red pepper, ginger, and tangerine peel to skillet and cook, stirring, until vegetables are tender-crisp, 3 minutes. Transfer to large bowl.

3. In same skillet, heat 2 teaspoons oil over medium-high heat; add half of beef and cook, stirring, until lightly browned, 2 minutes. Use slotted spoon to transfer beef to bowl with broccoli mixture as it is browned. Repeat with remaining 2 teaspoons oil and beef.

4. Add juice mixture to skillet and heat to boiling; boil 1 minute. Return vegetables and beef to skillet; heat through.

Each serving: About 350 calories, 26 g protein, 20 g carbohydrate, 18 g total fat (6 g saturated), 4 g fiber, 59 mg cholesterol, 525 mg sodium.

North African Flank Steak

PREP 5 minutes plus standing   **COOK** 16 minutes   **MAKES** 4 main-dish servings

1 teaspoon ground coriander	1/2 teaspoon salt
1 teaspoon ground cumin	1/4 teaspoon ground cinnamon
1 teaspoon paprika	1 beef flank steak (11/4 pounds)
1 teaspoon dried thyme	2 teaspoons vegetable oil
1/2 teaspoon coarsely ground black pepper	

1. In small bowl, combine coriander, cumin, paprika, thyme, pepper, salt, and cinnamon. Rub spice mixture all over steak. Place steak on plate; let stand at room temperature 15 minutes. Meanwhile, in nonstick 10-inch skillet, heat oil over medium-high heat until hot but not smoking.

2. Add steak to skillet and cook 7 to 8 minutes per side for medium-rare or until desired doneness.

3. Transfer steak to cutting board. To serve, thinly slice steak diagonally against the grain.

Each serving: About 315 calories, 44 g protein, 1 g carbohydrate, 14 g total fat (5 g saturated), 1 g fiber, 74 mg cholesterol, 365 mg sodium.

Vegetable Stir-Fry

PREP 20 minutes **COOK** 18 minutes **MAKES** 4 accompaniment servings

Start with this basic recipe, then add other ingredients to suit your taste. Possibilities include Asian (toasted) sesame oil, thinly sliced radishes, hot chiles, crushed red pepper, or soy sauce.

1   tablespoon vegetable oil
2   garlic cloves, thinly sliced
1   teaspoon minced, peeled fresh ginger
1   small bunch broccoli (12 ounces), cut into flowerets (about 3 cups)
1   cup water
1   cup peeled and thinly sliced carrots

1   yellow pepper, cut into 1/2-inch pieces
6   mushrooms, trimmed and thinly sliced
3   green onions, cut on diagonal into 1-inch pieces
2   tablespoons hoisin sauce
1/4 teaspoon salt

In nonstick 12-inch skillet, heat oil over medium-high heat until hot. Add garlic and ginger and cook, stirring frequently (stir-frying), 1 minute. Add broccoli, and stir-fry 1 minute. Increase heat to high; add water and cook 3 minutes. Add carrots and yellow pepper, and stir-fry until liquid has evaporated, about 6 minutes. Add mushrooms, green onions, hoisin sauce, and salt; stir-fry until vegetables are tender and almost all liquid has evaporated, about 5 minutes longer.

Each serving: About 109 calories, 4 g protein, 15 g carbohydrate, 4 g total fat (1 g saturated), 2 g fiber, 0 mg cholesterol, 355 mg sodium.

Steak au Poivre

PREP 10 minutes   **COOK** 15 minutes   **MAKES** 4 main-dish servings

1   tablespoon whole black
     peppercorns, crushed
1/2 teaspoon salt
4   beef tenderloin steaks (filet
     mignon), 1¹/4 inches thick
     (5 ounces each)
1   tablespoon butter or
     margarine

1   tablespoon olive oil
1/4 cup dry white wine
2   tablespoons brandy
1/2 cup heavy or whipping cream
1   tablespoon chopped fresh
     chives

1. In cup, mix peppercorns and salt. Rub mixture all over steaks.

2. In nonstick 12-inch skillet, melt butter with oil over medium-high heat. Add steaks and cook 7 to 8 minutes per side for medium-rare or until desired doneness. Transfer steaks to four dinner plates; keep warm.

3. Add wine and brandy to skillet; heat to boiling, stirring, until browned bits are loosened from bottom of skillet. Add cream, and boil about 1 minute or until sauce thickens. Stir in chopped chives. Pour sauce over steaks.

Each serving: About 579 calories, 26 g protein, 2 g carbohydrate, 50 g total fat (22 g saturated), 0 g fiber, 149 mg cholesterol, 399 mg sodium.

Sautéed Mixed Mushrooms

PREP 15 minutes **COOK** 10 minutes **MAKES** 4 accompaniment servings

This classic French preparation brings out the meaty texture and woodsy flavor of mushrooms. Use just one variety, if you prefer.

2   tablespoons butter or
    margarine
1/4 cup minced shallots
8   ounces white mushrooms,
    trimmed and cut into quarters
4   ounces shiitake mushrooms,
    stems removed and caps cut
    into 1-inch-thick wedges
4   ounces oyster mushrooms,
    cut in half if large

1/4 teaspoon salt
1/8 teaspoon ground black
    pepper
1/8 teaspoon dried thyme
1   small garlic clove, finely
    chopped
1   tablespoon chopped fresh
    parsley

In 12-inch skillet, melt butter over medium-high heat. Add shallots and cook, 1 minute. Stir in white, shiitake, and oyster mushrooms. Sprinkle with salt, pepper, and thyme and cook, stirring, until mushrooms are tender and liquid has evaporated, about 8 minutes longer. Stir in garlic and parsley and cook 1 minute longer.

Each serving: About 86 calories, 3 g protein, 7 g carbohydrate, 6 g total fat (4 g saturated), 2 g fiber, 16 mg cholesterol, 207 mg sodium.

Chile Steak with Avocado-Tomato Salad

PREP 15 minutes **COOK** 5 minutes **MAKES** 4 main-dish servings

Chile Steak

- 2 chipotle chiles in adobo*, finely chopped
- 2 garlic cloves, crushed with press
- 2 tablespoons honey
- 2 teaspoons fresh lime juice
- 1 teaspoon dried oregano, crushed
- 3/4 teaspoon salt
- 1/4 teaspoon coarsely ground pepper
- 1 beef skirt steak (1 1/4 pounds)

Avocado-Tomato Salad

- 1 pint red or yellow cherry tomatoes, each cut in half
- 1 ripe avocado, pitted, peeled, and cut into 3/4-inch chunks
- 1 tablespoon coarsely chopped fresh cilantro leaves
- 2 teaspoons fresh lime juice
- 1/8 teaspoon salt

1. Prepare Chile Steak: In cup, mix chipotles, garlic, honey, and lime juice; set aside.

2. In another cup, mix oregano, salt, and pepper; rub all over steak.

3. Heat ridged grill pan over medium-high heat until very hot. Place steak in pan; brush top with half of chipotle mixture and cook 2 minutes. Turn steak over; brush with remaining mixture and cook 2 to 3 minutes longer for medium-rare or until desired doneness. Turn steak over again; cook 30 seconds. Transfer steak to cutting board; keep warm.

4. Meanwhile, prepare Avocado-Tomato Salad: In bowl, mix tomatoes, avocado, cilantro, lime juice, and salt. Makes about 3 cups.

5. Thinly slice steak; serve with avocado salad.

See note on page 29.

Each serving steak: About 310 calories, 35 g protein, 13 g carbohydrate, 12 g total fat (4 g saturated), 0 g fiber, 108 mg cholesterol, 865 mg sodium.
Each 1/2 cup avocado salad: About 65 calories, 1 g protein, 5 g carbohydrate, 5 g total fat (1 g saturated), 2 g fiber, 0 mg cholesterol, 55 mg sodium.

Pork and Lamb

Spicy Ground Lamb and Vegetable Kabobs with Herbed Yogurt Sauce

PREP 35 minutes **BROIL** 10 minutes **MAKES** 4 main-dish servings

Herbed Yogurt Sauce
- 1 cup plain low-fat yogurt
- 2 tablespoons minced fresh dill
- 2 tablespoons minced fresh cilantro
- 1 tablespoon minced fresh oregano leaves (optional)
- 1 tablespoon fresh lemon juice
- 1/8 teaspoon salt

Lamb and Vegetable Kabobs
- 1 pound ground lamb
- 2 green onions, minced
- 2 garlic cloves, crushed with garlic press
- 1 jalapeño chile, seeded and minced

- 2 tablespoons minced fresh cilantro
- 2 teaspoons grated peeled fresh ginger
- 1/2 teaspoon ground coriander
- 1/2 teaspoon ground cumin
- 11/4 teaspoons salt
- 3/8 teaspoon ground black pepper
- 1 medium Japanese eggplant (5 ounces)
- 1 medium red onion
- 1 medium green or red pepper
- 1 large portobello mushroom (6 ounces), stem discarded
- 1 tablespoon olive oil
- 4 long all-metal skewers

1. Prepare Herbed Yogurt Sauce: In small serving bowl, stir yogurt with dill, cilantro, oregano, if using, lemon juice, and salt. Cover and refrigerate until ready to serve. Makes about 1 cup.

2. Preheat broiler. Prepare Lamb and Vegetable Kabobs: In medium bowl, combine lamb, green onions, garlic, jalapeño, cilantro, ginger, coriander, cumin, 3/4 teaspoon salt, and 1/4 teaspoon black pepper just until well blended but not overmixed; set aside. Cut eggplant, red onion, green pepper, and mushroom into 8 pieces each. Toss vegetables with oil, remaining 1/2 teaspoon salt, and 1/8 teaspoon black pepper.

3. On each skewer, thread 2 pieces of each vegetable. Shape one-fourth of lamb mixture around remaining length of each skewer. Place skewers on rack in broiling pan. Place pan in broiler at closest position to source of

heat and broil skewers until lamb is cooked through and vegetables are lightly browned and tender, 10 minutes, turning once. Serve lamb and vegetables with yogurt sauce.

Each serving lamb and vegetables: About 325 calories, 24 g protein, 11 g carbohydrate, 20 g total fat (7 g saturated), 4 g fiber, 83 mg cholesterol, 805 mg sodium. Each tablespoon sauce: About 10 calories, 1 g protein, 1 g carbohydrate, 0 g total fat, 0 g fiber, 1 mg cholesterol, 30 mg sodium.

Smart Carbs

Cajun Ham Steak

PREP 5 minutes **COOK** 8 minutes **MAKES** 4 main-dish servings

Here is an ideal supper for busy weeknights. It boasts a super-short shopping list and is on the table in less than forty minutes.

2 **teaspoons Cajun seasoning blend**	1 **fully cooked smoked ham steak, 1/2 inch thick (1 1/4 pounds)**
1/2 **teaspoon sugar**	**lime wedges**

1. Heat ridged grill pan or heavy skillet over medium-high heat until very hot but not smoking. In small bowl, combine Cajun seasoning and sugar. Rub seasoning mixture on both sides of ham steak.

2. Place ham steak in grill pan and cook until heated through and lightly browned, about 4 minutes per side. Serve with lime wedges.

Each serving: About 135 calories, 25 g protein, 1 g carbohydrate, 5 g total fat (2 g saturated), 0 g fiber, 68 mg cholesterol, 1,980 mg sodium.

Corn and Red Pepper Salsa

PREP 15 minutes   **COOK** 5 minutes   **MAKES** 2 cups

4   ears corn, husks and silk removed, or 1 bag (10 ounces) frozen whole-kernel corn, thawed
2   tablespoons fresh lime juice
2   tablespoons chopped fresh cilantro leaves

1   tablespoon olive oil
1/4   teaspoon salt
1   medium red pepper, cut into 1/4-inch pieces
1   green onion, thinly sliced

1. If using fresh corn, with sharp knife, cut kernels from cobs. In 4-quart saucepan, heat *2 inches water* to boiling over high heat. Add corn and heat to boiling; boil 30 seconds. Drain. Rinse with cold running water and drain well.

2. In medium bowl, with wire whisk, mix lime juice, cilantro, oil, and salt until blended. Add corn, red pepper, and green onion; toss until mixed and coated with dressing.

Each 1/4 cup: About 60 calories, 2 g protein, 10 g carbohydrate, 2 g total fat (0 g saturated), 2 g fiber, 0 mg cholesterol, 80 mg sodium.

Garlicky Spinach

PREP 5 minutes   **COOK** 5 minutes   **MAKES** 4 accompaniment servings

1   tablespoon olive oil
1   large garlic clove, minced

2   bags (10 ounces each) fresh spinach, rinsed and drained but not spun dry, tough stems trimmed
1/4   teaspoon salt

In 12-inch skillet, heat oil over medium-high heat until hot. Add garlic and cook, stirring, until fragrant, 30 seconds. Stir in half the spinach with water clinging to leaves; cover and cook just until wilted, 2 minutes. Add remaining spinach and cook, uncovered, until tender, 2 minutes longer. Stir in salt.

Each serving: About 60 calories, 4 g protein, 5 g carbohydrate, 4 g total fat (1 g saturated), 4 g fiber, 0 mg cholesterol, 245 mg sodium.

Curried Pork Medallions

PREP 5 minutes **COOK** 10 minutes **MAKES** 4 main-dish servings

A simple skillet dinner: Tender slices of pork are flavored with curry and apple, then tossed with baby carrots.

1 bag (16 ounces) peeled baby carrots
1 tablespoon olive oil
1 medium Gala or Golden Delicious apple, unpeeled, cored, and cut into 1/2-inch cubes
2 teaspoons curry powder

1 garlic clove, crushed with garlic press
1 pork tenderloin (1 pound), trimmed and cut into 3/4-inch-thick slices
1/2 teaspoon salt
1/4 cup apple cider or apple juice

1. Place carrots in covered microwavable dish with *1/4 cup water*. Cook in microwave oven on High until carrots are tender, about 6 minutes.

2. Meanwhile, in nonstick 12-inch skillet, heat oil over medium-high heat. Add apple, curry powder, and garlic; cook, stirring, 1 minute.

3. Add pork and salt, and cook until pork is still slightly pink in center, 6 to 8 minutes. Add cider and cooked carrots with any liquid, and heat to boiling; cook 1 minute.

Each serving: About 250 calories, 25 g protein, 17 g carbohydrate, 9 g total fat
(2 g saturated), 3 g fiber, 71 mg cholesterol, 390 mg sodium.

Middle Eastern Lamb Steaks

PREP 15 minutes **COOK** 20 minutes **MAKES** 4 main-dish servings

Aromatic spices—coriander, cumin, and allspice—in a quick tomato relish add zip to simple pan-seared lamb steaks.

1 **teaspoon dried thyme**	1 **medium red onion, chopped**
1 **teaspoon ground coriander**	1/4 **cup dried currants**
1 **teaspoon ground cumin**	1 **tablespoon pine nuts**
1/2 **teaspoon ground allspice**	**(optional)**
1/2 **teaspoon salt**	2 **tablespoons chopped fresh**
1/4 **teaspoon ground black pepper**	**parsley leaves**
1 **can (28 ounces) whole tomatoes**	2 **center-cut lamb leg steaks,**
	3/4 **inch thick (8 ounces**
	each), trimmed
1 **teaspoon vegetable oil**	

1. In small bowl, stir together thyme, coriander, cumin, allspice, salt, and pepper. Drain tomatoes, reserving 1/2 cup juice; chop tomatoes.

2. In nonstick 12-inch skillet, heat oil over medium heat until hot. Add onion and 2 teaspoons thyme mixture. Cook, stirring occasionally, until onion is slightly softened, 5 minutes. Add chopped tomatoes, reserved juice, and currants. Cook, stirring occasionally, until slightly thickened, 6 minutes. Transfer tomato mixture to bowl; stir in pine nuts, if using, and 1 tablespoon parsley.

3. Coat lamb steaks with remaining thyme mixture. In same skillet, cook lamb over medium-high heat 4 to 5 minutes per side for medium-rare or until of desired doneness. Cut each steak in half.

4. To serve, spoon tomato relish into deep platter; top with lamb and sprinkle with remaining 1 tablespoon parsley.

Each serving: About 255 calories, 26 g protein, 17 g carbohydrate, 9 g total fat (3 g saturated), 3 g fiber, 78 mg cholesterol, 555 mg sodium.

SERVING SUGGESTION
Sautéed zucchini and summer squash.

Apricot-Mustard Glazed Ham

PREP 15 minutes   **BAKE** 1 hour 30 minutes   **MAKES** 10 main-dish servings

This beautifully glistening ham is a worthy centerpiece for any spring entertaining menu.

1 **fully cooked smoked bone-in shank-half ham (7 pounds)**	1/3 **cup apricot preserves** 1 **tablespoon Dijon mustard**

1. Preheat oven to 325°F. If necessary, with sharp knife, remove skin and trim fat from ham, leaving about 1/4-inch-thick layer of fat. Place ham in medium roasting pan (14" by 10"). Bake ham 1 hour.

2. In small bowl, stir apricot preserves and mustard until blended.

3. Remove ham from oven; brush with glaze. Return to oven and bake until meat thermometer inserted in thickest part of ham without touching bone reaches 130°F, about 25 to 30 minutes longer. Internal temperature of ham will rise 5° to 10°F upon standing.

4. Transfer ham to warm platter and let stand 15 minutes to set juices for easier slicing.

Each serving: About 235 calories, 31 g protein, 8 g carbohydrate, 8 g total fat (3 g saturated), 0 g fiber, 71 mg cholesterol, 1,750 mg sodium.

Chilled Buttermilk-Vegetable Soup

PREP 20 minutes plus chilling   **MAKES** about 10 cups or 10 first-course servings

The refreshing, cool flavors of summer vegetables make this chunky soup a delightful first course.

2 limes	1 ripe avocado, pitted, peeled, and cut into 1/4-inch cubes
1 1/2 quarts buttermilk (6 cups)	1 cup loosely packed fresh cilantro leaves, chopped
3 medium tomatoes (1 pound), seeded and cut into 1/4-inch cubes	1 teaspoon salt
1 English (seedless) cucumber, unpeeled and cut into 1/4-inch cubes	1/4 teaspoon coarsely ground black pepper

1. From limes, grate 1 teaspoon peel and squeeze 3 tablespoons juice.

2. In large bowl, stir lime peel and juice with buttermilk, tomatoes, cucumber, avocado, cilantro, salt, and pepper until blended. Cover and refrigerate at least 2 hours or up to 24 hours.

Each serving: About 105 calories, 6 g protein, 11 g carbohydrate, 4 g total fat (1 g saturated), 2 g fiber, 5 mg cholesterol, 395 mg sodium.

Cuban Mojo Pork Chops

PREP 15 minutes plus marinating   **GRILL** 15 minutes   **MAKES** 4 main-dish servings

Mojo (pronounced MO-ho) comes from the Spanish verb *mojar*, to wet. The seasoning mix is an integral component of Latin cuisine, whether used as a condiment or as a base for a marinade. It traditionally was made with citrus juice, garlic, salt, and lard (now vegetable oil), but newly added ingredients such as spices, herbs, onion, chiles, and even fruit make it extremely versatile.

2 **medium oranges**	2 **tablespoons fresh lime juice**
1/4 **cup chopped onion**	1/4 **teaspoon salt**
1/4 **cup red wine vinegar**	4 **pork loin chops, 3/4 inch**
1 **chipotle chile in adobo* plus**	**thick (8 ounces each),**
1 **tablespoon adobo**	**trimmed**
4 **garlic cloves**	

1. From oranges, grate 1/2 teaspoon peel and squeeze 1/2 cup juice.

2. In blender or food processor with knife blade attached, pulse orange peel, onion, vinegar, chipotle chile, adobo, and garlic until pureed.

3. Pour marinade into large zip-tight plastic bag; stir in orange and lime juices and salt. Add pork chops to marinade, turning to coat. Seal bag, pressing out excess air. Place bag on plate; let stand 15 minutes at room temperature or 1 hour in the refrigerator, turning over several times.

4. Prepare charcoal fire or preheat gas grill for covered direct grilling over medium heat.

5. Remove chops from bag; pour marinade into 1-quart saucepan and reserve. Place chops on hot grill rack. Cover grill and grill chops until lightly browned on the outside and still slightly pink on the inside, 6 to 8 minutes per side.

6. Meanwhile, heat reserved marinade to boiling over high heat; boil 2 minutes.

7. Serve pork chops drizzled with cooked marinade.

See note on page 29.

Each serving: About 395 calories, 42 g protein, 10 g carbohydrate, 19 g total fat
(7 g saturated), 1 g fiber, 116 mg cholesterol, 410 mg sodium.

Spinach Salad with Orange

PREP 10 minutes   **MAKES** 4 first-course servings

3 large navel oranges	1/4 teaspoon ground black pepper
2 tablespoons extravirgin olive oil	2 bags (5 ounces each) baby spinach
1/2 teaspoon salt	

1. From 1 of the oranges, grate 1 teaspoon peel and squeeze 6 tablespoons juice. With knife, cut peel and white pith from remaining oranges. Slice oranges crosswise in half, then cut each half into 1/4-inch-thick slices; set slices aside.

2. In medium bowl, whisk orange peel and juice with oil, salt, and pepper. Add spinach; toss to coat.

3. To serve, place spinach mixture on four salad plates; top with orange.

Each serving: About 110 calories, 3 g protein, 11 g carbohydrate, 7 g total fat
(1 g saturated), 8 g fiber, 0 mg cholesterol, 375 mg sodium.

Butterflied Lamb with Moroccan Flavors

PREP 15 minutes plus marinating   **GRILL** 15 to 25 minutes
MAKES 12 main-dish servings

Fabulous exotic flavor with very little work.

1/3 cup loosely packed fresh cilantro leaves, chopped	1 teaspoon salt
1/4 cup olive oil	1/2 teaspoon coarsely ground black pepper
2 tablespoons dried mint	1/2 teaspoon chili powder
2 teaspoons ground coriander	31/2 pounds butterflied boneless lamb leg, trimmed*
1 teaspoon ground ginger	

1. In small bowl, stir cilantro, oil, mint, coriander, ginger, salt, pepper, and chili powder.

2. Place lamb in 13" by 9" baking dish. Rub lamb with cilantro mixture to coat completely. Cover and refrigerate at least 1 hour or up to 4 hours.

3. Prepare charcoal fire or preheat gas grill for covered direct grilling over medium-low heat.

4. Place lamb on hot grill rack. Cover grill and grill lamb 15 to 25 minutes for medium-rare or until desired doneness, turning lamb occasionally. Thickness of butterflied lamb will vary throughout; cut off sections of lamb as they are cooked and place on cutting board.

5. Let lamb stand 10 minutes to allow juices to set for easier slicing. Thinly slice lamb to serve.

Ask butcher to debone a 41/2-pound lamb leg shank half and slit the meat lengthwise to spread open like a thick steak.

Each serving: About 225 calories, 28 g protein, 1 g carbohydrate, 12 g total fat (3 g saturated), 0 g fiber, 88 mg cholesterol, 270 mg sodium.

Chunky Greek Salad

PREP 30 minutes **MAKES** about 8 cups or 12 accompaniment servings

2 tablespoons extravirgin olive oil

2 tablespoons fresh lemon juice

3/4 teaspoon salt

1/2 teaspoon coarsely ground black pepper

1 pint grape tomatoes, each cut in half

6 Kirby cucumbers (1 1/2 pounds), unpeeled and cut into 1" by 1/2" chunks

1 large red pepper, cut into 1-inch pieces

1 green onion, thinly sliced

1/2 cup kalamata olives, pitted and coarsely chopped

1/4 cup loosely packed fresh mint leaves, chopped

3 ounces feta cheese, crumbled (3/4 cup; optional)

1. In large serving bowl, with fork, combine oil, lemon juice, salt, and black pepper.

2. Add tomatoes, cucumbers, red pepper, green onion, olives, and mint. Toss until evenly mixed. If not serving right away, cover and refrigerate up to 6 hours. Sprinkle with feta, if you like, to serve. Toss before serving.

Each serving: About 45 calories, 1 g protein, 5 g carbohydrate, 3 g total fat (0 g saturated), 2 g fiber, 0 mg cholesterol, 195 mg sodium.

Jerk Pork Chops with Grilled Pineapple

PREP 15 minutes **GRILL** 12 minutes **MAKES** 4 main-dish servings

We love this shortcut Jamaican jerk—made with thick, juicy pork and succulent fruit. Try our jerk rub on chicken pieces or salmon steaks too.

1 baby pineapple or 1/2 regular pineapple
1 lime
2 tablespoons jerk seasoning*
1 tablespoon olive oil

4 pork loin chops, 3/4 inch thick (8 ounces each), trimmed
   lime wedges (optional)

1. Prepare charcoal fire or preheat gas grill for direct grilling over medium heat.

2. With sharp knife, cut pineapple lengthwise through crown to stem end in 4 wedges, leaving on leafy crown.

3. From lime, grate 1/2 teaspoon peel and squeeze 1 tablespoon juice. In small bowl, mix lime peel and juice with jerk seasoning and oil. Rub both sides of pork chops with jerk mixture.

4. Place pork chops on hot grill rack and grill until browned on the outside and still slightly pink on the inside, 10 to 12 minutes, turning once. While chops are cooking, add pineapple wedges, cut sides down, to same grill; cook 5 minutes, turning wedges over once. Transfer chops and pineapple to same platter. Serve with lime wedges, if you like.

Seasoning mixes vary among manufacturers, especially with regard to salt content. Add salt to taste if necessary.

Each serving: About 400 calories, 41 g protein, 8 g carbohydrate, 22 g total fat (7 g saturated), 1 g fiber, 116 mg cholesterol, 535 mg sodium.

Pork Chops with Peppers and Onions

PREP 10 minutes   **COOK** 20 minutes   **MAKES** 4 main-dish servings

Boneless chops are smothered in green onions and red peppers for this fast and easy skillet dinner.

4 boneless pork loin chops, 1/2 inch thick (4 ounces each), trimmed	2 medium red peppers, cut into 11/2-inch pieces
1/2 teaspoon salt	1 garlic clove, crushed with garlic press
1/4 teaspoon ground black pepper	1/8 teaspoon crushed red pepper
2 teaspoons olive oil	1/2 cup chicken broth
1 bunch green onions, green tops cut diagonally into 3-inch pieces, white bottoms thinly sliced crosswise	

1. Heat nonstick 12-inch skillet over medium-high heat until hot but not smoking. Add pork chops to skillet and sprinkle with salt and pepper. Cook chops until lightly browned on the outside and still slightly pink on the inside, about 8 minutes, turning once (reduce heat to medium if chops are browning too quickly). Transfer chops to plate; keep warm.

2. To skillet, add oil and green-onion tops; cook 4 minutes. With slotted spoon, transfer green-onion tops to small bowl. In same skillet, cook red peppers and green-onion bottoms, stirring occasionally, 8 minutes. Add garlic and crushed red pepper, and cook, stirring, 1 minute. Stir in broth and half of green-onion tops; heat through. Spoon pepper mixture onto platter; top with chops and remaining green-onion tops.

Each serving: About 210 calories, 26 g protein, 7 g carbohydrate, 8 g total fat
(2 g saturated), 2 g fiber, 71 mg cholesterol, 495 mg sodium.

Asparagus and Endive Salad with Orange-Mustard Vinaigrette

PREP 15 minutes **COOK** 5 minutes **MAKES** 4 accompaniment servings

This light salad is an "elegant-but-easy" accompaniment to a weeknight meal.

1 pound asparagus, trimmed and cut diagonally into 2" by 1/4" slices	1/2 teaspoon sugar
	1/2 teaspoon salt
1 orange	1/2 teaspoon Dijon mustard
2 tablespoons seasoned rice vinegar	1/8 teaspoon ground black pepper
1 tablespoon olive oil	2 heads Belgian endive (4 ounces each), cut lengthwise into 1/4-inch-wide strips
1 tablespoon minced shallot	

1. In 12-inch skillet, heat *1/2 inch water* to boiling over high heat. Add asparagus and cook until tender-crisp, 3 minutes. Drain asparagus in colander; rinse with cold water and pat dry.

2. Meanwhile, from orange, grate 1/2 teaspoon peel and squeeze 1 tablespoon juice. In small bowl, with wire whisk, whisk orange peel and juice with vinegar, oil, shallot, sugar, salt, mustard, and pepper until blended.

3. To serve, toss asparagus and endive in large bowl with dressing until evenly coated.

Each serving: About 85 calories, 3 g protein, 10 g carbohydrate, 4 g total fat (1 g saturated), 4 g fiber, 0 mg cholesterol, 540 mg sodium.

Spice-Brined Pork Loin

PREP 20 minutes plus 18 to 24 hours chilling and brining
ROAST 1 hour to 1 hour 15 minutes   **MAKES** 12 main-dish servings

Brining pork in a blend of kosher salt, sugar, and spices infuses it with wonderful flavor and keeps it tender and juicy. Allow the pork to soak in the brine for 18 to 24 hours before roasting.

1/4 cup sugar	peel from 1 navel orange, white pith removed
1/4 cup kosher salt	
2 tablespoons coriander seeds	1 boneless pork loin roast (3 pounds), trimmed
2 tablespoons cracked black pepper	4 garlic cloves, crushed with side of chef's knife
2 tablespoons fennel seeds	
2 tablespoons cumin seeds	

1. In 2-quart saucepan, heat *1 cup water* with sugar, salt, coriander, pepper, fennel, cumin, and orange peel to boiling over high heat. Reduce heat to low; simmer 2 minutes. Remove saucepan from heat; stir in *3 cups ice* until almost melted. Stir in *1 cup cold water*.

2. Place pork in large zip-tight plastic bag with garlic and brine. Seal bag, pressing out excess air. Place bag in bowl or small roasting pan and refrigerate 18 to 24 hours.

3. Preheat oven to 400°F. Remove pork from bag; discard brine (it's OK if some spices stick to pork). Place pork on rack in medium roasting pan (14" by 10"). Roast until thermometer inserted into thickest part reaches 150°F, about 1 hour to 1 hour 15 minutes (temperature will rise 5° to 10°F upon standing). Transfer pork to cutting board and let stand 10 minutes to set juices for easier slicing.

Each serving: About 175 calories, 24 g protein, 1 g carbohydrate, 8 g total fat (3 g saturated), 0 g fiber, 67 mg cholesterol, 445 mg sodium.

Pickled Green Beans

PREP 30 minutes plus chilling   **COOK** 5 minutes
MAKES about 13 cups or 12 accompaniment servings

This twist on a favorite summer vegetable is reminiscent of the popular Dilly Beans of the 1960s.

	salt	2	teaspoons dill seeds
3	pounds green beans, ends trimmed	2	teaspoons mustard seeds
2/3	cup sugar	1 1/2	cups distilled white vinegar
3	garlic cloves, peeled	1/2	cup loosely packed fresh dill, chopped

1. In 8-quart saucepot, heat *5 quarts salted water* to boiling over high heat. Add green beans and cook until tender-crisp, 5 to 7 minutes. Drain beans in large colander; rinse under cold running water to stop cooking.

2. In 2-quart saucepan, heat sugar, garlic cloves, dill seeds, mustard seeds, *1/2 cup vinegar*, 2 teaspoons salt, and *1/2 cup water* to boiling over medium-high heat; cook 1 minute, stirring to dissolve sugar. Remove saucepan from heat; add remaining 1 cup vinegar and *1 1/2 cups cold water*; stir to combine.

3. Place green beans in jumbo (2-gallon) zip-tight plastic bag. Pour vinegar mixture over beans. Seal bag, pressing out excess air. Place bag in 13" by 9" pan and refrigerate 24 hours or up to 5 days, turning bag occasionally.

4. To serve, drain beans and toss with chopped dill.

Each serving: About 45 calories, 2 g protein, 11 g carbohydrate, 0 g total fat, 3 g fiber, 0 mg cholesterol, 200 mg sodium.

Chile-Rubbed Ham with Peach Salsa

PREP 30 minutes   **GRILL** 5 minutes   **MAKES** 4 main-dish servings

It's an easy grill—a fully cooked ham steak is quickly patted with paprika and smoky chiles before searing. Our soothing salsa tames the spice.

Peach Salsa
- 4 ripe peaches (1¹/4 pounds), pitted and cut into ¹/4-inch cubes
- 1 cup loosely packed fresh cilantro leaves, chopped
- 1 jalapeño chile, seeded and minced
- 2 tablespoons peach jam
- 2 tablespoons fresh lime juice
- ¹/4 teaspoon salt

Chile-Rubbed Ham
- 1 tablespoon paprika
- 1 tablespoon olive oil
- 2 teaspoons minced chipotle chile in adobo* or 2 teaspoons adobo sauce
- 1 fully cooked center-cut ham steak, ¹/2 inch thick (1¹/4 pounds)

1. Prepare Peach Salsa: In medium bowl, toss together peaches, cilantro, jalapeño, jam, lime juice, and salt. Cover and refrigerate salsa up to 1 day if not serving right away. Makes about 4 cups.

2. Prepare charcoal fire or preheat gas grill for direct grilling over medium-high heat.

3. Prepare Chile-Rubbed Ham: In cup, mix paprika, oil, and chipotle chile. Spread mixture on both sides of ham.

4. Place ham on hot grill rack. Grill until lightly browned and heated through, 4 to 6 minutes, turning once. Serve ham with salsa.

See note on page 29.

Each serving ham: About 180 calories, 24 g protein, 1 g carbohydrate, 8 g total fat (2 g saturated), 0 g fiber, 72 mg cholesterol, 1,820 mg sodium.
Each ¹/2 cup salsa: About 40 calories, 0 g protein, 10 g carbohydrate, 0 g total fat, 2 g fiber, 0 mg cholesterol, 80 mg sodium.

SERVING SUGGESTION
A salad of baby greens garnished with slices of avocado.

Gruyère and Mushroom Crepes

PREP 20 minutes **BAKE** 5 minutes **MAKES** 4 main-dish servings

Using a package of store-bought crepes makes this dish a breeze to put together.

1 **pound cremini mushrooms, sliced**	1 **package (4.5 ounces) French-style crepes (each 7 inches in length)**
1/3 **cup half-and-half or light cream**	8 **thin slices deli-baked ham (4 ounces)**
1/4 **teaspoon salt**	6 **ounces Gruyère or Swiss cheese, shredded (11/2 cups)**
1/4 **teaspoon coarsely ground black pepper**	

1. Heat nonstick 12-inch skillet over medium heat until hot. Add mushrooms and cook, stirring occasionally, until browned and tender, about 7 minutes. Add half-and-half, *1/4 cup water*, salt, and pepper and cook 1 minute longer, stirring. Transfer mushroom mixture to small bowl.

2. Preheat oven to 400°F. Place 8 crepes on work surface, browned side down (reserve remaining 2 crepes for another use). On each crepe, place 1 slice ham; sprinkle with 2 tablespoons Gruyère and top with scant 1/4 cup mushroom mixture. Gently roll each crepe, jelly-roll fashion, to enclose filling. Place rolled crepes in shallow oven-safe ceramic platter or broiling pan. Sprinkle with remaining 1/2 cup Gruyère. Bake crepes until hot and edges are lightly browned, 5 minutes.

Each serving: About 345 calories, 27 g protein, 10 g carbohydrate, 21 g total fat (11 g saturated), 3 g fiber, 111 mg cholesterol, 835 mg sodium.

SERVING SUGGESTION
A tossed salad.

Orange Pork and Asparagus Stir-Fry

PREP 20 minutes   **COOK** 6 minutes   **MAKES** 4 main-dish servings

Slices of lean pork tenderloin are quickly cooked with fresh asparagus and juicy orange pieces.

2 navel oranges
1 teaspoon olive oil
1 pork tenderloin (12 ounces), trimmed, thinly sliced diagonally
3/4 teaspoon salt
1/4 teaspoon ground black pepper

1 1/2 pounds thin asparagus, trimmed and each stalk cut in half
1 garlic clove, crushed with garlic press

1. From 1 orange, grate 1 teaspoon peel and squeeze 1/4 cup juice. Cut off peel and white pith from remaining orange. Cut orange into 1/4-inch slices; cut each slice into quarters.

2. In nonstick 12-inch skillet, heat 1/2 teaspoon oil over medium-high heat until hot but not smoking. Add half the pork and sprinkle with 1/4 teaspoon salt and 1/8 teaspoon pepper. Cook, stirring frequently, until pork just loses its pink color, 2 minutes. Transfer pork to plate. Repeat with remaining 1/2 teaspoon oil, pork, 1/4 teaspoon salt, and remaining 1/8 teaspoon pepper. Transfer pork to same plate.

3. To same skillet, add asparagus, garlic, orange peel, remaining 1/4 teaspoon salt, and 1/4 cup water; cover and cook, stirring occasionally, until asparagus is tender-crisp, about 2 minutes. Return pork to skillet. Add orange juice and orange pieces; heat through, stirring often.

Each serving: About 165 calories, 24 g protein, 8 g carbohydrate, 4 g total fat (1 g saturated), 2 g fiber, 50 mg cholesterol, 495 mg sodium.

Spicy Garlic Lamb with Cucumber Raita

PREP 30 minutes plus chilling **GRILL** 15 to 25 minutes **MAKES** 8 main-dish servings

Leg of lamb isn't only for the oven; it's divine cooked on the grill. The cucumbers in a minted yogurt dressing balance the spicy meat.

Cucumber Raita
- 6 Kirby cucumbers (1¹/2 pounds)
- 1 teaspoon salt
- 2 cups plain low-fat yogurt
- ¹/2 cup loosely packed fresh mint leaves, chopped
- 1¹/2 teaspoons sugar

Spiced Lamb
- 1 tablespoon fennel seeds
- 1 tablespoon mustard seeds

- 1 tablespoon cumin seeds
- 2 teaspoons salt
- 1 teaspoon whole black peppercorns
- 1 teaspoon dried thyme leaves
- 3 whole cloves
- 3 garlic cloves, crushed with garlic press
- 2 tablespoons fresh lemon juice
- 3¹/2 pounds butterflied boneless lamb leg, trimmed*

1. Prepare Cucumber Raita: With vegetable peeler, remove several strips of peel from each cucumber. Cut each cucumber lengthwise in half; scoop out seeds. Cut each half lengthwise in half, then crosswise into ¹/2-inch-thick pieces. In medium bowl, toss cucumbers with ¹/4 teaspoon salt; let stand 10 minutes. With hand, press cucumbers to remove as much liquid as possible; drain off liquid. Stir in yogurt, mint, sugar, and remaining ³/4 teaspoon salt. Cover and refrigerate until ready to serve or up to 6 hours. Makes about 4 cups.

2. Prepare charcoal fire or preheat gas grill for covered direct grilling over medium-low heat.

3. Prepare Spiced Lamb: In spice grinder or coffee grinder, blend fennel, mustard, cumin, salt, peppercorns, thyme, and cloves until finely ground. In small bowl, mix garlic and lemon juice with ground spices until blended. Rub spice mixture over both sides of lamb.

4. Place lamb on hot grill rack. Cover and grill 15 to 25 minutes for medium-rare or until desired doneness, turning lamb over once. Thickness of butterflied lamb will vary throughout; cut off sections of

lamb as they are cooked and place on cutting board. Let lamb stand 10 minutes to set juices for easier slicing. Thinly slice lamb and arrange on platter. Serve with Cucumber Raita.

Ask butcher to debone a 4 1/2-pound lamb leg shank half and slit the meat lengthwise to spread open like a thick steak.

Each serving lamb: About 275 calories, 39 g protein, 2 g carbohydrate, 11 g total fat (4 g saturated), 1 g fiber, 121 mg cholesterol, 675 mg sodium.
Each 1/2 cup raita: About 60 calories, 4 g protein, 10 g carbohydrate, 2 g total fat (0 g saturated), 2 g fiber, 4 mg cholesterol, 260 mg sodium.

Honey-Glazed Spiral-Cut Ham

PREP 15 minutes   **BAKE** 1 hour 15 minutes   **MAKES** 16 servings

You can't beat the ease of this delicious ham topped with our creamy, piquant sauce. It comes presliced around the bone and is available in most supermarkets as well as by mail order.

1/2 **fully cooked smoked spiral-cut ham (8 pounds)**

3/4 **cup packed dark brown sugar**

3 **tablespoons honey**

1 **tablespoon Dijon mustard**

1. Preheat oven to 350°F. In small roasting pan (13" by 9"), place ham flat side down. Cover loosely with foil and bake 45 minutes.

2. Meanwhile, in small bowl, mix brown sugar, honey, mustard, and *1 tablespoon water* until blended.

3. Remove foil and brush ham all over with glaze. Bake 30 minutes longer, brushing ham occasionally with drippings in roasting pan.

Each serving: About 260 calories, 32 g protein, 14 g carbohydrate, 8 g total fat (3 g saturated), 0 g fiber, 74 mg cholesterol, 1,740 mg sodium.

Creamy Mustard and Dill Sauce

PREP 15 minutes **MAKES** about 2 cups

This lemony dill sauce has just a hint of mustard. Save any leftover sauce to spread on sandwiches another day.

1	lemon	1/4	cup low-fat (1%) milk
1 1/4	cups reduced-fat sour cream	2	tablespoons Dijon mustard
3/4	cup light mayonnaise	1	teaspoon sugar
1/2	cup loosely packed fresh dill, chopped	1/4	teaspoon coarsely ground black pepper

1. From lemon, grate 1 teaspoon peel and squeeze 2 tablespoons juice.

2. In small bowl, mix lemon peel and juice with sour cream, mayonnaise, dill, milk, mustard, sugar, and pepper until blended. Cover and refrigerate until ready to serve or up to 3 days.

Each tablespoon: About 35 calories, 0 g protein, 2 g carbohydrate, 3 g total fat (1 g saturated), 0 g fiber, 6 mg cholesterol, 45 mg sodium.

Collards with Pickled Red Onions

PREP 35 minutes plus chilling **COOK** 15 minutes
MAKES about 6 cups or 16 accompaniment servings

Bright pink, sweet-and-sour red onions are a perfect complement to peppery green collards.

2 medium red onions, thinly sliced	2 tablespoons olive oil
1/3 cup red wine vinegar	1/4 teaspoon crushed red pepper
2 tablespoons sugar	5 pounds collard greens, stems
3/4 teaspoon salt	removed and discarded,
1/8 teaspoon coarsely ground black pepper	leaves coarsely chopped

1. In 3-quart saucepan, heat *8 cups water* to boiling over high heat. Add onion slices and heat to boiling; cook 2 minutes. Drain onions. Rinse onions with cold running water; drain well.

2. Meanwhile, in medium bowl, mix vinegar, sugar, 1/4 teaspoon salt, and pepper until blended. Add onions and toss to mix. Cover and refrigerate onions at least 4 hours or up to 24 hours.

3. About 20 minutes before serving, in 8-quart saucepot, heat oil and crushed red pepper over medium-high heat until hot. Gradually add collard greens and cook, stirring frequently, until wilted and tender, 10 to 15 minutes. Stir in remaining 1/2 teaspoon salt.

4. To serve, transfer collard greens to serving bowl. With slotted spoon, remove pickled onions from bowl and arrange over greens.

**Each serving: About 50 calories, 2 g protein, 7 g carbohydrate, 2 g total fat
(0 g saturated), 3 g fiber, 0 mg cholesterol, 105 mg sodium.**

BBQ Pork Chops

PREP 10 minutes   **COOK** 20 minutes   **MAKES** 4 main-dish servings

For a smokier flavor, cook chops in a covered grill.

1	tablespoon olive oil	2	tablespoons light or dark molasses
4	bone-in pork loin or rib chops, 3/4 inch thick (8 ounces each)	2	tablespoons brown sugar
1	medium onion, chopped	1/8	teaspoon ground red pepper (cayenne)
1	cup marinara sauce		
1/4	cup red wine vinegar		

1. In nonstick 12-inch skillet, heat oil over medium-high heat until very hot but not smoking. Add chops and cook until browned on both sides, 6 minutes. Transfer chops to plate.

2. Add onion to skillet; cook, covered, until lightly browned, 2 minutes. Stir in marinara sauce, vinegar, molasses, brown sugar, and ground red pepper.

3. Reduce heat to medium-low; add chops to skillet. Cover and simmer, until pork is cooked through and sauce thickens, 12 to 14 minutes, turning chops once. Juices will run clear when chop is pierced with tip of knife.

Each serving: About 575 calories, 36 g protein, 15 g carbohydrate, 40 g total fat (13 g saturated), 2 g fiber, 110 mg cholesterol, 430 mg sodium.

Shredded Carrots

The fastest way to cook carrots and also one of the best. Add a pinch each of cloves and ginger for a spicier dish, if you like.

4	carrots, peeled and shredded (2 cups)	2	tablespoons butter or margarine
2	tablespoons water	1	teaspoon sugar
		1/2	teaspoon salt

In small saucepan, combine carrots, water, butter, sugar, and salt; heat to boiling over high heat. Reduce heat; cover and simmer, stirring occasionally, until carrots are tender, 3 to 4 minutes.

Each serving: About 78 calories, 1 g protein, 7 g carbohydrate, 6 g total fat
(4 g saturated), 2 g fiber, 16 mg cholesterol, 367 mg sodium.

Maple-Glazed Pork Tenderloins

PREP 10 minutes plus refrigerating   **GRILL** 20 minutes   **MAKES** 6 main-dish servings

2	pork tenderloins (12 ounces each), trimmed	8	wooden toothpicks
1/2	teaspoon salt	6	slices bacon
1/4	teaspoon ground black pepper	1/2	cup maple or maple-flavor syrup

1. Sprinkle tenderloins with salt and pepper. Place pork in bowl; cover and refrigerate 30 minutes.

2. Meanwhile, soak toothpicks in water for 30 minutes. Prepare charcoal fire or preheat gas grill for covered direct grilling over medium heat.

3. Wrap 3 bacon slices around each tenderloin and secure with toothpicks. Place tenderloins on grill and grill, brushing frequently with maple syrup and turning over occasionally, until meat thermometer inserted in center of pork reaches 155°F, 20 to 25 minutes. Internal temperature of pork will rise to 160°F upon standing. Transfer pork to cutting board and let stand 5 minutes to set juices for easier slicing.

Each serving: About 265 calories, 28 g protein, 18 g carbohydrate, 9 g total fat
(3 g saturated), 86 mg cholesterol, 350 mg sodium.

Roasted Cauliflower

PREP 10 minutes   **ROAST** 23 minutes   **MAKES** 6 accompaniment servings

Cauliflower becomes lightly browned and tender-crisp when roasted. It's a delicious change from the familiar boiled version.

1   **medium head cauliflower (2 pounds), cut into 1 1/2" flowerets**
1   **tablespoon olive oil**
1/2   **teaspoon salt**

1/4   **teaspoon coarsely ground black pepper**
2   **tablespoons chopped fresh parsley**
1   **garlic clove, finely chopped**

1. Preheat oven to 450°F. In jelly-roll pan, toss cauliflower, oil, salt, and pepper until evenly coated. Roast until cauliflower is tender, about 20 minutes, stirring halfway through roasting.

2. In small cup, combine parsley and garlic. Sprinkle over cauliflower and stir to mix evenly. Roast 3 minutes longer. Spoon into serving dish.

Each serving: About 35 calories, 1 g protein, 3 g carbohydrate, 2 g total fat (0 g saturated), 4 g fiber, 0 mg cholesterol, 202 mg sodium.

Sesame Pork Tenderloins

PREP 15 minutes **ROAST** 30 minutes **MAKES** 6 main-dish servings

Whole pork tenderloins are brushed with a flavorful mixture of hoisin sauce, ginger, and sesame oil, then coated with sesame seeds and roasted until golden.

1/4 **cup hoisin sauce**
1 **tablespoon grated, peeled fresh ginger**
1/2 **teaspoon Asian sesame oil**

1/3 **cup sesame seeds**
2 **whole pork tenderloins (3/4 pound each)**

1. Preheat oven to 475°F. In small bowl, with wire whisk, whisk hoisin sauce, ginger, and sesame oil until blended.

2. Spread sesame seeds in even layer on waxed paper. With pastry brush, spread hoisin mixture all over tenderloins; roll in sesame seeds to coat.

3. Place tenderloins on rack in small roasting pan; tuck small ends under to help cook evenly. Roast 15 minutes; turn tenderloins over and roast until still slightly pink in center, about 15 minutes longer. (Internal temperature of meat should be 155°F on meat thermometer and will rise 5° upon standing.)

4. Place tenderloins on cutting board; let stand 5 minutes to set juices for easier slicing. Holding knife at an angle, thinly slice tenderloins.

Each serving: About 215 calories, 26 g protein, 7 g carbohydrate, 9 g total fat (2 g saturated), 1 g fiber, 68 mg cholesterol, 220 mg sodium.

SERVING SUGGESTION
A side dish of brown rice or warm whole-wheat tortillas as wraps with green onion and cucumber.

Pork Chops with Tomato and Arugula

PREP 10 minutes   **COOK** 5 minutes   **MAKES** 4 main-dish servings

1/3	cup plain dried bread crumbs	2	tablespoons olive oil
1/4	cup grated Romano cheese	1	tablespoon fresh lemon juice
1	teaspoon salt	1	large ripe tomato (12 ounces)
1	large egg	1/2	small red onion
4	boneless pork loin chops, 1/2-inch thick (4 ounces each)	1	bag (4 to 5 ounces) baby arugula

1. On waxed paper, combine bread crumbs, Romano, and 1/2 teaspoon salt. In pie plate, with fork, beat egg. Dip chops, one at a time, in egg, then in bread-crumb mixture to coat. Repeat with remaining chops.

2. In nonstick 12-inch skillet, heat 1 tablespoon oil over medium-high heat. Add chops and cook until cooked through, 5 to 6 minutes, turning chops once. Juices will run clear when chop is pierced with tip of knife.

3. Meanwhile, in medium bowl, combine lemon juice and remaining 1 tablespoon oil and 1/2 teaspoon salt. Coarsely chop tomato; thinly slice onion. Toss arugula, onion, and tomato with dressing in bowl.

4. Transfer chops to four dinner plates; top with salad.

Each serving: About 370 calories, 31 g protein, 14 g carbohydrate, 22 g total fat (6 g saturated), 2 g fiber, 128 mg cholesterol, 800 mg sodium.

Pork and Posole Stew

PREP 45 minutes **COOK** 1 hour 45 minutes
MAKES about 10 cups or 10 main-dish servings

This is the Southwestern version of a traditional Mexican pork-and-hominy stew that's often served as a festive meal over the holidays. A staple of the Southwest's Pueblo Indians, posole—or hominy—is made with white or yellow corn kernels treated with slaked lime or lye until the kernels are doubled in size. They're then degermed, hulled, washed, and dried. Our recipe uses convenient ready-to-eat canned hominy.

3　teaspoons olive oil
3　pounds boneless pork shoulder blade roast (fresh pork butt), trimmed and cut into 2-inch chunks
1/2　(7-ounce) jar roasted red peppers, drained*
1/4　teaspoon ground red pepper (cayenne)
2　large onions, chopped
4　garlic cloves, crushed with garlic press
2　jalapeño chiles, seeded and minced

1　can (14 1/2 ounces) whole tomatoes with their juice
1 1/2　teaspoons salt
1　teaspoon dried oregano
1/4　teaspoon coarsely ground black pepper
1　can (29 ounces) hominy, rinsed and drained
　　sliced radishes, cilantro leaves, and diced avocado for garnish

1. In nonstick 5- or 6-quart saucepot or Dutch oven, heat 1 teaspoon olive oil over medium-high heat until very hot. Add pork chunks in batches, and cook until browned on all sides, about 8 minutes, stirring often. With slotted spoon, transfer pork to bowl as it is browned. Repeat with remaining pork, using 1 teaspoon olive oil per batch; set aside.

2. Meanwhile, place roasted red peppers in blender along with ground red pepper; blend until pureed.

3. To same saucepot, add onions, garlic, and jalapeños, and cook until vegetables are tender, stirring occasionally, about 10 minutes.

4. Return pork to saucepot. Add tomatoes with their juice, salt, oregano, black pepper, pureed red-pepper mixture, and *1 cup water*; heat to boiling over medium-high heat, breaking up tomatoes with side of spoon. Reduce heat to low; cover and simmer until meat is fork-tender and cooked through, stirring occasionally, about 1 hour 30 minutes.

5. Stir in hominy; cover and cook until heated through, about 15 minutes longer. Garnish each serving with radishes, cilantro, and avocado.

Or, if you prefer, you can substitute 1 large red pepper, seeded, roasted, and peeled, for the jarred roasted red peppers.

Each serving: About 255 calories, 24 g protein, 14 g carbohydrate, 11 g total fat (3 g saturated), 3 g fiber, 77 mg cholesterol, 620 mg sodium.

Kansas City Ribs

PREP 1 hours 15 minutes   **GRILL** 15 minutes   **MAKES** 6 main-dish servings

Baby back ribs with a gooey tomato-based sauce are a summertime tradition, whether you enjoy them as a main dish or serve them as an appetizer.

Ribs
3   racks pork baby back ribs
     (1 pound each)
1   onion, cut into quarters
1   orange, cut into quarters
1   tablespoon whole black
     peppercorns
1   tablespoon whole coriander
     seeds

Barbecue Sauce
3   tablespoons butter or margarine
1   medium onion, chopped
4   garlic cloves, finely chopped
1   can (15 ounces) tomato sauce
1/4 cup cider vinegar
1/4 cup packed brown sugar
1   teaspoon salt
1/4 teaspoon coarsely ground
     black pepper

1. Prepare Ribs: In 8-quart saucepot, place ribs, onion, orange, peppercorns, coriander, and enough *water* to cover; heat to boiling over high heat. Reduce heat to low; partially cover and cook 50 minutes to 1 hour or until ribs are fork-tender. Transfer ribs to platter. If not serving right away, cover and refrigerate until ready to serve.

2. Meanwhile, prepare Barbecue Sauce: In 2-quart saucepan, heat butter over medium heat until melted. Add onion and garlic and cook until softened, stirring occasionally, 8 minutes. Add tomato sauce, vinegar, sugar, salt, and pepper; heat to boiling over high heat. Reduce heat to low; simmer until thickened, stirring occasionally, 40 minutes. Makes about 2 2/3 cups.

3. Prepare charcoal fire or preheat gas grill for covered direct grilling over medium heat.

4. Place ribs on hot grill rack. Cover grill and grill ribs until browned, 8 to 10 minutes, turning once. Brush ribs with some sauce and grill 5 to 10 minutes longer, brushing with remaining sauce and turning frequently.

5. To serve, cut racks into 1-rib portions and arrange on platter.

**Each serving: About 390 calories, 21 g protein, 16 g carbohydrate, 27 g total fat
(11 g saturated), 2 g fiber, 94 mg cholesterol, 943 mg sodium.**

Mediterranean Grilled Eggplant
and Summer Squash

PREP 15 minutes   **GRILL** 10 minutes   **MAKES** 6 accompaniment servings

This summertime recipe can be served hot or cool and doubles easily. If you're feeding a crowd, grill the vegetables in batches.

3   tablespoons olive oil
2   tablespoons red wine vinegar
2   teaspoons Dijon mustard
1   garlic clove, crushed with garlic press
1/4   teaspoon salt
1/4   teaspoon coarsely ground black pepper
1   medium zucchini (8 ounces), cut lengthwise into 1/4-inch-thick slices

1   medium yellow squash (8 ounces), cut lengthwise into 1/4-inch-thick slices
1   small eggplant (11/4 pounds), cut lengthwise into 1/4-inch-thick slices
2   tablespoons chopped fresh mint
1   ounce ricotta salata or feta cheese, crumbled (1/4 cup)

1. Prepare charcoal fire or preheat gas grill for direct grilling over medium heat. Prepare vinaigrette: In small bowl, with wire whisk, mix oil, vinegar, mustard, garlic, salt, and pepper until blended; brush on one side of vegetable slices.

2. Place zucchini, yellow squash, and eggplant, vinaigrette side down, on grill. Grill, turning once and brushing with remaining vinaigrette, until browned and tender, 10 to 15 minutes. Transfer vegetables to large platter as they are done.

3. To serve, sprinkle vegetables with mint and ricotta salata.

Each serving: About 114 calories, 3 g protein, 9 g carbohydrate, 8 g total fat
(2 g saturated), 4 g fiber, 4 mg cholesterol, 222 mg sodium.

Sopressata and Roma Bean Salad with Pecorino

PREP 10 minutes   **COOK** 8 minutes   **MAKES** 4 main-dish servings

This antipasto-style salad is hearty enough to make a great meal.

1¹/4 pounds Roma (broad) beans or green beans, trimmed	4 ounces thinly sliced sopressata or Genoa salami, cut into ¹/2-inch-wide strips
1 lemon	2 bunches arugula (4 ounces each), tough stems discarded
2 tablespoons extravirgin olive oil	1 wedge Pecorino Romano cheese (2 ounces)
¹/4 teaspoon salt	
¹/8 teaspoon coarsely ground black pepper	

1. If Roma beans are very long, cut crosswise into 2¹/2-inch pieces. In 12-inch skillet, heat *1 inch water* to boiling over high heat. Add beans; heat to boiling. Reduce heat to low; simmer until beans are tender-crisp, 6 to 8 minutes. Drain beans. Rinse with cold running water to stop cooking; drain again.

2. Meanwhile, from lemon, grate ¹/2 teaspoon peel and squeeze 2 tablespoons juice. In large bowl, with wire whisk, mix lemon peel and juice with oil, salt, and pepper.

3. Add beans, sopressata, and arugula to dressing in bowl; toss to coat.

4. To serve, spoon salad onto platter. With vegetable peeler, shave thin strips from wedge of Pecorino to top salad.

Each serving: About 280 calories, 14 g protein, 14 g carbohydrate, 21 g total fat (7 g saturated), 5 g fiber, 41 mg cholesterol, 845 mg sodium.

Seafood

Shrimp Saté with Cucumber Salad

PREP 45 minutes plus marinating   **GRILL** 5 minutes   **MAKES** 4 main-dish servings

8 (7-inch) bamboo skewers	2 small cucumbers (8 ounces each)
1 tablespoon vegetable oil	2 tablespoons sugar
6 tablespoons fresh lime juice (3 to 4 limes)	1 tablespoon snipped fresh chives
3 tablespoons minced fresh cilantro	2 tablespoons slivered fresh basil leaves
1/2 teaspoon salt	3 tablespoons chopped roasted salted peanuts
1/2 teaspoon crushed red pepper	
1 pound large shrimp, shelled and deveined	

1. Prepare charcoal fire or preheat gas grill for direct grilling over medium heat.

2. Soak skewers in water to cover for 30 minutes. Drain before using.

3. While skewers soak, in medium bowl, with wire whisk, whisk together oil, 3 tablespoons lime juice, 2 tablespoons cilantro, 1/4 teaspoon salt, and 1/4 teaspoon crushed red pepper. Stir in shrimp and marinate at room temperature 15 minutes.

4. Meanwhile, prepare cucumber salad: Cut each unpeeled cucumber lengthwise in half. With spoon, scoop out seeds. Thinly slice cucumber halves crosswise. In another medium bowl, with rubber spatula, stir cucumbers, sugar, chives, 1 tablespoon basil, remaining 3 tablespoons lime juice, 1 tablespoon cilantro, 1/4 teaspoon salt, and 1/4 teaspoon crushed red pepper. Set aside. Makes about 3 cups.

5. Thread about 4 shrimp on each skewer. Lightly oil shrimp. Place skewers on hot rack. Grill shrimp until just opaque throughout, 4 to 5 minutes, turning once.

6. Spoon cucumber salad onto four dinner plates; sprinkle with peanuts. Arrange skewers with shrimp over salad. Sprinkle with remaining 1 tablespoon basil.

Each serving: About 205 calories, 22 g protein, 13 g carbohydrate, 8 g total fat (1 g saturated), 2 g fiber, 180 mg cholesterol, 555 mg sodium.

Shrimp Étouffée

PREP 20 minutes   **COOK** 45 minutes   **MAKES** 4 main-dish servings

Étouffée means "smothered" in Cajun French. In this skillet dinner, shrimp is smothered with a delicious seasoned tomato sauce.

1	tablespoon butter or margarine	1	bay leaf
2	tablespoons all-purpose flour	3/4	teaspoon chili powder
1	large red pepper, chopped	1/2	teaspoon salt
1	large onion, chopped	1/4	teaspoon dried thyme
2	medium celery stalks, thinly sliced	1/4	teaspoon ground red pepper (cayenne)
2	garlic cloves, crushed with garlic press	1	pound large shrimp, shelled and deveined
1	bottle (8 ounces) clam juice	3	green onions, thinly sliced
2	tablespoons tomato paste	1/2	cup loosely packed fresh parsley leaves, chopped

1. In nonstick 12-inch skillet, melt butter over medium heat. Stir in flour and cook, stirring frequently, until golden brown, 4 minutes. Add red pepper, onion, celery, and garlic and cook, stirring occasionally, 5 minutes.

2. Stir in clam juice, tomato paste, bay leaf, chili powder, salt, thyme, ground red pepper, and *1/2 cup water*. Heat to boiling over medium-high heat. Reduce heat to medium-low and simmer, covered, until vegetables are tender, 25 minutes.

3. Add shrimp, green onions, and parsley; simmer, covered, until shrimp turn opaque throughout, 8 minutes.

Each serving: About 211 calories, 26 g protein, 16 g carbohydrate, 5 g total fat
(3 g saturated), 3 g fiber, 180 mg cholesterol, 684 mg sodium.

SERVING SUGGESTION
Spoon over a mound of brown rice.

Skate with Brown Butter, Lemon, and Capers

PREP 15 minutes **COOK** 8 minutes **MAKES** 4 main-dish servings

1 tablespoon vegetable oil	1/3 cup loosely packed fresh parsley leaves, chopped
1/4 cup all-purpose flour	
2 skinless skate wings (10 ounces each), filleted	1/4 cup fresh lemon juice
	2 tablespoons drained capers
1/2 teaspoon salt	
3 tablespoons butter (no substitutions)	

1. In nonstick 12-inch skillet, heat oil over medium-high heat until very hot but not smoking. Place flour on waxed paper. Sprinkle skate fillets with salt, then coat with flour, shaking off excess. Add skate to skillet and cook until golden brown on the outside and just opaque throughout, about 4 minutes, turning once. Transfer skate to platter; keep warm.

2. Add butter to skillet and cook until foamy and light brown. Add parsley, lemon juice, and capers; swirl to combine. Pour over skate to serve.

Each serving: About 265 calories, 32 g protein, 6 g carbohydrate, 13 g total fat (5 g saturated), 0 g fiber, 25 mg cholesterol, 625 mg sodium.

Skate wings are the pectoral fins of a fish similar to a ray (the whole fish is rarely eaten). Each wing contains two layers of meat separated by a layer of cartilage. When the cartilage is removed, you will have two thin fillets. If skate is not available, you can substitute other delicately flavored, moderately firm-fleshed fillets, such as flounder, ocean perch, orange roughy, pompano, or red snapper.

Skillet Asparagus

PREP 10 minutes   **COOK** 12 minutes   **MAKES** 4 accompaniment servings

A splash of lime juice and a pinch of lime zest bring out the fresh flavor of succulent asparagus spears.

1	lime	1/4	teaspoon salt
1	tablespoon butter or margarine	1/8	teaspoon ground black pepper
1 1/2	pounds asparagus, trimmed		

1. From lime, grate 1/2 teaspoon peel and squeeze 1 tablespoon juice.

2. In nonstick 12-inch skillet, melt butter over medium-high heat. Add asparagus, lime juice, and *1/4 cup water*; heat to boiling. Reduce heat to medium and cook, covered, 5 minutes.

3. Add salt, pepper, and lime peel to skillet. Increase heat to medium-high; cook, uncovered, until asparagus is tender and liquid evaporates, 4 to 5 minutes.

Each serving: About 56 calories, 3 g protein, 3 g carbohydrate, 4 g total fat (3 g saturated), 1 g fiber, 8 mg cholesterol, 209 mg sodium.

Thai Snapper

PREP 20 minutes   **GRILL** 6 minutes   **MAKES** 4 main-dish servings

3 tablespoons fresh lime juice
1 tablespoon Asian fish sauce
1 tablespoon olive oil
1 teaspoon grated peeled fresh ginger
1/2 teaspoon sugar
1 small garlic clove, minced
4 red snapper fillets (6 ounces each)

1 large carrot, cut into 2¹/4-inch-long matchstick-thin strips
1 large green onion, thinly sliced
1/4 cup packed fresh cilantro leaves

1. Prepare charcoal fire or preheat gas grill for covered direct grilling over medium heat.

2. Meanwhile, in small bowl, mix lime juice, fish sauce, oil, ginger, sugar, and garlic. From roll of foil, cut four 16" by 12" sheets. Fold each sheet crosswise in half and open up again.

3. Just before grilling, assemble packets: Place 1 red snapper fillet, skin side down, on half of each piece of foil. Top with carrot, green onion, then cilantro leaves. Spoon lime-juice mixture over snapper and vegetables. Fold other half of foil over fish; fold and crimp foil edges all around to create 4 sealed packets.

4. Place packets on hot grill rack. Cover grill and grill 6 to 8 minutes, depending on thickness of snapper. Do not turn packets over.

5. Before serving, with kitchen shears, cut an X in top of each packet to let steam escape, then carefully pull back foil to open. When packets are open, check that fish is opaque throughout and flakes easily when tested with fork.

Each serving: About 230 calories, 36 g protein, 5 g carbohydrate, 6 g total fat (1 g saturated), 1 g fiber, 63 mg cholesterol, 270 mg sodium.

Gingery Japanese Eggplant

PREP 10 minutes plus marinating   **GRILL** 12 minutes   **MAKES** 4 accompaniment servings

Straight-from-a-Japanese-restaurant taste, prepared with ingredients from the supermarket.

1/3 cup teriyaki sauce
  1 tablespoon brown sugar
  1 tablespoon vegetable oil
  1 tablespoon rice vinegar
  2 teaspoons minced peeled
     fresh ginger

  4 small Japanese eggplants
     (4 ounces each), each cut
     lengthwise in half

1. In 13" by 9" baking dish, stir teriyaki sauce, brown sugar, oil, vinegar, and ginger until mixed.

2. With knife, lightly score cut side of eggplants in crisscross pattern, about 3/4-inch apart, being careful not to cut all the way through to skin. Place eggplants in marinade, cut sides down, and let stand 45 minutes at room temperature.

3. Meanwhile, prepare charcoal fire or preheat gas grill for covered direct grilling over medium heat.

4. Place eggplants, cut sides down, on hot grill rack, reserving marinade. Cover grill and grill eggplants 9 minutes. Turn eggplants over; brush with some reserved marinade and cook until tender and just beginning to char, about 3 minutes longer. Transfer eggplants to platter; drizzle with any remaining marinade.

Each serving: About 95 calories, 3 g protein, 14 g carbohydrate, 4 g total fat
(0 g saturated), 3 g fiber, 0 mg cholesterol, 915 mg sodium.

Mediterranean Grilled Sea Bass

PREP 10 minutes plus marinating   **GRILL** 12 minutes   **MAKES** 4 main-dish servings

The firm white flesh of sea bass holds up very well on the grill. If you can't get sea bass, substitute red snapper or striped bass.

2	lemons	2	whole sea bass (1¹/2
3	tablespoons olive oil		pounds each), cleaned and
1	tablespoon chopped fresh		scaled
	oregano leaves	¹/4	teaspoon ground black
1	teaspoon ground coriander		pepper
1¹/4	teaspoons salt	2	large oregano sprigs

1. Prepare charcoal fire or preheat gas grill for covered direct grilling over medium heat.

2. Meanwhile, from 1 lemon, grate 1 tablespoon peel and squeeze 2 tablespoons juice. Cut half of remaining lemon into slices, the other half into wedges. In small bowl, stir lemon juice and peel with oil, chopped oregano, coriander, and ¹/4 teaspoon salt.

3. Rinse fish and pat dry with paper towels. Make 3 slashes in both sides of each fish. Sprinkle inside and out with pepper and remaining 1 teaspoon salt. Place lemon slices and oregano sprigs inside fish cavities. Place fish in 13" by 9" baking dish. Rub half of oil mixture over outsides of fish; reserve remaining oil mixture to drizzle over cooked fish. Let stand at room temperature 15 minutes.

4. Lightly oil fish; place on hot rack. Cover and grill until fish just turns opaque throughout when knife is inserted at backbone, 12 to 14 minutes, turning once.

5. To serve, place fish on cutting board. Working with 1 fish at a time, with knife, cut along backbone from head to tail. Slide cake server under front section of top fillet and lift off from backbone; transfer to platter. Slide server under backbone and lift away from bottom fillet; discard. Slide cake server between bottom fillet and skin, and transfer fillet to platter. Repeat with second fish. Drizzle fillets with the remaining oil mixture. Serve with lemon wedges.

Each serving: About 305 calories, 40 g protein, 1 g carbohydrate, 15 g total fat (3 g saturated), 0 g fiber, 90 mg cholesterol, 730 mg sodium.

Zucchini Ribbons with Mint

PREP 10 minutes **COOK** 4 minutes **MAKES** 4 accompaniment servings

Making long, paper-thin strips of zucchini is an out-of-the-ordinary way to prepare it. If you don't have fresh mint, use parsley instead.

4	small zucchini (4 ounces each) or 2 medium zucchini (8 ounces each)	1/2	teaspoon salt
1	tablespoon olive oil	2	tablespoons chopped fresh mint
2	garlic cloves, crushed with side of chef's knife		

1. Trim ends from zucchini. With vegetable peeler, peel long thin ribbons from each zucchini.

2. In 12-inch skillet, heat oil over medium heat. Add garlic and cook until golden; discard garlic. Increase heat to high. Add zucchini and salt and cook, stirring, just until zucchini wilts, about 2 minutes. Remove from heat and stir in mint.

Each serving: About 49 calories, 1 g protein, 4 g carbohydrate, 4 g total fat (0 g saturated), 2 g fiber, 0 mg cholesterol, 294 mg sodium.

Dilled Tuna-Stuffed Tomatoes

PREP 25 minutes **MAKES** 4 main-dish servings

Substituting reduced-fat mayonnaise for the full-fat version will cut the amount of fat by 6 grams per serving. You won't miss the fat, and the tuna mixture retains its creamy consistency.

- 2 Kirby cucumbers, unpeeled and cut into 1/4-inch pieces
- 1/4 cup loosely packed fresh dill, finely chopped
- 1/4 cup mayonnaise
- 2 tablespoons capers, finely chopped
- 2 tablespoons fresh lemon juice
- 1 tablespoon Dijon mustard
- 1/4 teaspoon ground black pepper
- 2 cans (6 ounces each) solid white tuna in water, drained
- 4 ripe large tomatoes (12 ounces each)

1. In medium bowl, combine cucumbers, dill, mayonnaise, capers, lemon juice, mustard, pepper, and tuna, flaking tuna with fork.

2. Cut each tomato, from blossom end, into 6 attached wedges, being careful not to cut all the way through. Spoon one-fourth of tuna mixture into center of each tomato.

Each serving: About 255 calories, 18 g protein, 14 g carbohydrate, 14 g total fat (2 g saturated), 3 g fiber, 38 mg cholesterol, 515 mg sodium.

Glazed Salmon with Watermelon Salsa

PREP 20 minutes **GRILL** 10 minutes **MAKES** 4 main-dish servings

1 lime
4 cups (1/2-inch cubes) seedless watermelon (from 2 1/2-pound piece)
1/4 cup loosely packed fresh mint leaves, chopped
2 tablespoons chopped green onions

1 small jalapeño chile, seeded and finely chopped (1 tablespoon)
1/4 cup hoisin sauce
1/2 teaspoon Chinese five-spice powder
4 salmon steaks, 1 inch thick (6 ounces each)

1. Prepare charcoal fire or preheat gas grill for covered direct grilling over medium heat.

2. Meanwhile, prepare salsa: From lime, grate 1 teaspoon peel and squeeze 1 tablespoon juice. In serving bowl, toss lime peel and juice with watermelon, mint, green onions, and jalapeño. Makes about 3 2/3 cups.

3. In cup, stir hoisin sauce and five-spice powder.

4. Oil salmon, and place on hot grill rack. Brush salmon with half of hoisin mixture. Cover grill and grill salmon 3 minutes. Turn salmon over; brush with remaining hoisin mixture. Cover and grill 3 minutes. Turn salmon over again, and grill until salmon just turns opaque throughout, 3 minutes longer. Serve salmon with watermelon salsa.

Each serving: About 345 calories, 30 g protein, 18 g carbohydrate, 17 g total fat (3 g saturated), 2 g fiber, 81 mg cholesterol, 260 mg sodium.

Prepare this recipe any time of the year by substituting orange segments, sliced strawberries, or pineapple cubes for the melon.

Flounder Pesto Roll-Ups

PREP 15 minutes   **COOK** 20 minutes   **MAKES** 4 main-dish servings

Fresh fish fillets are spread with store-bought pesto and baked with white wine and plum tomatoes for a simply satisfying meal.

4 flounder fillets (6 ounces each)	4 plum tomatoes (3/4 pound), chopped
8 teaspoons refrigerated basil pesto	1/4 cup loosely packed fresh parsley leaves, chopped
1/4 teaspoon salt	
1/4 cup dry white wine	

1. Preheat oven to 400°F. Place fillets, skinned side down, on work surface. Spread 2 teaspoons pesto on each fillet; sprinkle with salt. Starting at narrow end of each fillet, roll up jelly-roll fashion. Place roll-ups, seam side down, in 8" by 8" baking dish.

2. Pour wine over fillets and top with tomatoes. Cover dish and bake until just opaque throughout, 20 minutes. Sprinkle with parsley to serve.

Each serving: About 205 calories, 31 g protein, 5 g carbohydrate, 6 g total fat (1 g saturated), 1 g fiber, 76 mg cholesterol, 335 mg sodium.

Fisherman's Stew

PREP 30 minutes **COOK** 25 minutes **MAKES** 4 main-dish servings

Fennel and tomato accent the seafood trio of monkfish, shrimp, and mussels. Double this one when company's coming—just make sure to use a large Dutch oven instead of a skillet.

2	teaspoons olive oil	1	can (14¹/2 ounces) diced
1	medium onion, chopped		tomatoes
1	medium fennel bulb	1	pound monkfish, dark
	(1 pound), trimmed, cored,		membrane and bones
	and thinly sliced		discarded (if any), or cod,
¹/2	teaspoon salt		cut into 1¹/4 -inch pieces
¹/8	teaspoon coarsely ground	1	pound mussels, scrubbed
	black pepper		and debearded
1	large lemon	¹/2	pound large shrimp, shelled
2	garlic cloves, crushed with		and deveined, leaving tail
	garlic press		part of shell on, if you like
1	bottle (8 ounces) clam juice	¹/2	cup loosely packed fresh
¹/2	cup dry white wine		parsley leaves, chopped

1. In deep nonstick 12-inch skillet, heat oil over medium-high heat until hot. Add onion, fennel, salt, and pepper; cook, covered, stirring occasionally, until vegetables are tender and golden, 10 minutes.

2. Meanwhile, from lemon, with vegetable peeler, remove 3 strips peel (3" by ³/4" each).

3. Add garlic to skillet and cook 30 seconds. Add clam juice, wine, and lemon peel; heat to boiling. Boil 1 minute. Reduce heat to medium-low; simmer, stirring occasionally, 5 minutes.

4. Stir in tomatoes with their juice; heat to boiling over medium-high heat. Add monkfish, mussels, and shrimp; heat to boiling. Reduce heat to medium-low and simmer, covered, until fish and shrimp turn opaque throughout and mussel shells open, 6 to 7 minutes. Remove lemon peel

and discard. Discard any mussels that have not opened. Sprinkle with parsley just before serving.

Each serving: About 265 calories, 34 g protein, 17 g carbohydrate, 6 g total fat (1 g saturated), 4 g fiber, 111 mg cholesterol, 1,145 mg sodium.

SERVING SUGGESTION
Whole-wheat pita wedges.

Smart Carbs

Cod with Cabbage

PREP 15 minutes   **COOK** 25 minutes   **MAKES** 4 main-dish servings

Cabbage is cooked with bacon and seasonings, then topped with cod in this easy four-ingredient dinner. You can substitute other firm white fish fillets such as orange roughy, pollock, or halibut for the cod.

2 slices bacon, chopped	1/2 teaspoon salt
1 small head savoy cabbage (2 pounds), thinly sliced (12 cups)	1/4 teaspoon coarsely ground black pepper
1/8 teaspoon dried thyme	4 cod fillets, 3/4 inch thick (6 ounces each)

1. In nonstick 12-inch skillet, cook bacon over medium heat, stirring frequently, until browned, about 5 minutes. With slotted spoon, transfer bacon to paper towels to drain. Discard all but 2 teaspoons bacon fat from skillet.

2. To same skillet, add cabbage, thyme, 1/4 teaspoon salt, 1/8 teaspoon pepper, and *2 tablespoons water*. Cook over medium-high heat, stirring frequently, until cabbage is wilted, 5 to 8 minutes. Stir in bacon.

3. Top cabbage mixture with cod fillets. Sprinkle cod with remaining 1/4 teaspoon salt and 1/8 teaspoon pepper. Cover skillet and cook over medium heat until cod is just opaque throughout, 10 to 12 minutes.

Each serving: About 235 calories, 36 g protein, 13 g carbohydrate, 5 g total fat (2 g saturated), 7 g fiber, 78 mg cholesterol, 490 mg sodium.

Mediterranean Swordfish Salad

PREP 10 minutes   **COOK** 10 minutes   **MAKES** 4 main-dish servings

Swordfish is a hearty addition to a quick cucumber salad.

3	tablespoons olive oil	1	English (seedless) cucumber (12 ounces), cut into 1/2-inch chunks
1	swordfish steak, 1 inch thick (11/4 pounds)		
1/4	teaspoon ground black pepper	1	pint grape or cherry tomatoes, each cut in half
3/4	teaspoon salt	11/3	ounces feta cheese, crumbled (1/3 cup)
2	tablespoons fresh lemon juice		
11/2	teaspoons chopped fresh oregano leaves or 1/2 teaspoon dried oregano		

1. In 10-inch skillet, heat 1 tablespoon oil over medium-high heat until very hot. Pat swordfish dry with paper towels. Add swordfish to skillet; sprinkle with pepper and 1/2 teaspoon salt. Cook until swordfish is browned on both sides and just turns opaque throughout, 10 to 12 minutes, turning once.

2. Meanwhile, in large bowl, combine lemon juice, oregano, and remaining 2 tablespoons oil and 1/4 teaspoon salt.

3. When swordfish is done, transfer to cutting board; trim and discard skin. Cut swordfish into 1-inch cubes. Add swordfish, cucumber, and tomatoes to dressing in bowl; toss gently to coat. Sprinkle with feta to serve.

Each serving: About 315 calories, 32 g protein, 8 g carbohydrate, 17 g total fat (5 g saturated), 2 g fiber, 68 mg cholesterol, 720 mg sodium.

Salad Niçoise

PREP 20 minutes   **COOK** 35 minutes   **MAKES** 6 main-dish servings

This salad is a classic summertime supper.

Parsley Vinaigrette
- 1/4 cup loosely packed fresh parsley leaves, chopped
- 1/4 cup red wine vinegar
- 3 tablespoons olive oil
- 1 teaspoon Dijon mustard
- 1/4 teaspoon salt
- 1/4 teaspoon ground black pepper

Salad
- 1 pound small red potatoes, not peeled
- 6 large eggs
- 1/2 pound green beans, trimmed and each cut crosswise in half
- 1 bag (5 ounces) mixed baby greens (8 cups loosely packed) or 1 head Boston lettuce, separated into leaves
- 1/2 English (seedless) cucumber, thinly sliced
- 1 can (12 ounces) solid white tuna in water, drained
- 1 pound tomatoes (3 medium), cut into wedges
- 1/2 cup niçoise olives (3 ounces)

1. Prepare Parsley Vinaigrette: In small bowl, with wire whisk, mix parsley, vinegar, oil, mustard, salt, and pepper until well blended; set aside.

2. Prepare Salad: In 3-quart saucepan, place potatoes and enough *water* to cover; heat to boiling over high heat. Reduce heat to low; simmer until potatoes are fork-tender, 10 to 12 minutes.

3. Meanwhile, in 2-quart saucepan, place eggs and enough *cold water* to cover by at least 1 inch; heat to boiling over high heat. Immediately remove saucepan from heat and cover tightly; let stand 15 minutes. Pour off hot water; run cold water over eggs to cool. Remove shells, and cut each egg into wedges.

4. When potatoes are done, with slotted spoon, remove potatoes from water to colander to drain. To same water in saucepan, add beans; heat to boiling over high heat. Reduce heat to low; simmer until tender-crisp, 5 to 10 minutes. Drain beans; rinse with cold running water to stop cooking; drain again.

5. In large bowl, toss greens with half of vinaigrette. Place greens on large platter. Cut each potato in half or into quarters if large; transfer to platter with greens. Arrange beans, eggs, cucumber, tuna, tomatoes, and olives in separate piles on same platter; drizzle with remaining vinaigrette.

Each serving: About 315 calories, 22 g protein, 24 g carbohydrate, 15 g total fat (3 g saturated), 4 g fiber, 233 mg cholesterol, 515 mg sodium.

Salmon with Tomato-Olive Relish

PREP 25 minutes   **GRILL** 8 minutes   **MAKES** 4 main-dish servings

Lightly season thick salmon steaks with herbes de Provence, a store-bought mix of dried herbs that's popular in southern France.

Tomato-Olive Relish
- 1 lemon
- 1/2 cup green olives, pitted and coarsely chopped
- 1 medium tomato, cut into 1/4-inch cubes
- 1 tablespoon minced red onion

Provençal Salmon
- 1 tablespoon fennel seeds, crushed
- 2 teaspoons herbes de Provence
- 1 teaspoon grated fresh orange peel
- 3/4 teaspoon salt
- 4 salmon steaks, 3/4 inch thick (6 ounces each)

1. Prepare Tomato-Olive Relish: From lemon, grate 1/2 teaspoon peel and squeeze 1 tablespoon juice. In medium bowl, toss lemon peel and juice with olives, tomato, and red onion. Cover and refrigerate relish up to 24 hours if not serving right away. Makes about 1 1/4 cups.

2. Prepare charcoal fire or preheat gas grill for covered direct grilling over medium heat.

3. Prepare Provençal Salmon: In cup, mix fennel, herbes de Provence, orange peel, and salt. Coat both sides of salmon with herb mixture.

4. Lightly oil salmon; place on hot rack. Grill salmon, carefully turning fish once with wide medal spatula, until just opaque throughout, 8 to 10 minutes. Serve salmon with relish.

Each serving salmon: About 270 calories, 29 g protein, 1 g carbohydrate, 16 g total fat (3 g saturated), 1 g fiber, 80 mg cholesterol, 515 mg sodium.
Each 1/4 cup relish: About 25 calories, 0 g protein, 3 g carbohydrate, 2 g total fat (0 g saturated), 1 g fiber, 0 mg cholesterol, 330 mg sodium.

Caesar Salad

2	anchovy fillets	1	tablespoon Dijon mustard
1	garlic clove, minced	1	teaspoon Worcestershire
1/4	cup mayonnaise		sauce
1/4	cup grated Romano cheese	1	bag (12 ounces) romaine
2	tablespoons fresh lemon		hearts, torn
	juice		freshly ground black pepper
1	tablespoon olive oil		

1. In large bowl, with fork, mash anchovies with garlic until almost smooth. Whisk in mayonnaise, Romano, lemon juice, oil, mustard, and Worcestershire until blended.

2. Add romaine to bowl with dressing; toss to coat. Sprinkle with pepper to taste.

Each serving: About 180 calories, 4 g protein, 5 g carbohydrate, 16 g total fat (3 g saturated), 1 g fiber, 15 mg cholesterol, 250 mg sodium.

Steamed Scrod Fillets

PREP 15 minutes **COOK** 10 minutes **MAKES** 4 main-dish servings

These fresh fillets are steamed on a bed of bok choy and carrots with a drizzle of ginger-soy mixture.

4 pieces scrod fillet (6 ounces each)
3 tablespoons reduced-sodium soy sauce
2 tablespoons seasoned rice vinegar
1 tablespoon finely chopped, peeled fresh ginger

1 garlic clove, crushed with garlic press
1 pound bok choy, coarsely chopped
1³/4 cups (half 10-ounce package) shredded carrots
3 green onions, sliced

1. With tweezers, remove any small bones from scrod fillets.

2. In small bowl, combine soy sauce, vinegar, ginger, and garlic.

3. Toss bok choy and carrots in 12-inch skillet. Fold thin ends of scrod fillets under to create even thickness. Place scrod over vegetables. Pour soy-sauce mixture over scrod; sprinkle with green onions.

4. Cover skillet and heat to boiling over high heat. Reduce heat to medium, and cook until scrod is just opaque throughout, about 10 minutes.

Each serving: About 200 calories, 34 g protein, 12 g carbohydrate, 2 g total fat (0 g saturated), 3 g fiber, 73 mg cholesterol, 820 mg sodium.

Roast Salmon with Capers and Tarragon

PREP 10 minutes   **ROAST** 30 minutes   **MAKES** 6 main-dish servings

A whole salmon fillet with a crusty crumb-and-herb topping looks festive, tastes fabulous, and is surprisingly quick and easy to prepare.

3 tablespoons butter or margarine	1 teaspoon dried tarragon, crumbled
1/3 cup plain dried bread crumbs	1/4 teaspoon salt
1/4 cup loosely packed fresh parsley leaves, minced	1/4 teaspoon coarsely ground black pepper
3 tablespoons drained capers, minced	1 whole salmon fillet (2 pounds)
2 teaspoons grated fresh lemon peel	lemon wedges

1. Preheat oven to 450°F.

2. In 1-quart saucepan, melt butter over low heat. Remove saucepan from heat; stir in bread crumbs, parsley, capers, lemon peel, tarragon, salt, and pepper.

3. Line 15½" by 10½" jelly-roll pan with foil; grease foil. Place salmon, skin side down, in pan and pat crumb mixture on top.

4. Roast until salmon is just opaque throughout and topping is lightly browned, 30 minutes. With two large spatulas, carefully transfer salmon to platter (it's OK if salmon skin sticks to foil). Serve with lemon wedges.

Each serving: About 325 calories, 28 g protein, 5 g carbohydrate, 21 g total fat (6 g saturated), 0 g fiber, 91 mg cholesterol, 407 mg sodium.

Mesclun Salad with Parmesan Polenta Rounds

PREP 20 minutes   **BROIL** 6 minutes   **MAKES** 6 first-course servings

Serve slices of polenta, broiled with Parmesan cheese and seasonings, over baby salad greens tossed with a creamy balsamic vinaigrette. A precooked polenta log from the supermarket that keeps for weeks in your fridge helps make this elegant first course a cinch to whip up.

1	log (16 ounces) precooked polenta, cut into 18 slices	1	tablespoon balsamic vinegar
1/2	cup coarsely grated Parmesan cheese	1	tablespoon olive oil
		1	tablespoon light mayonnaise
1/4	teaspoon dried thyme	1/2	teaspoon Dijon mustard
1/2	teaspoon salt	1/4	teaspoon sugar
1/2	teaspoon coarsely ground black pepper	2	bags (5 ounces each) mesclun salad greens
1	tablespoon white wine vinegar		

1. Preheat broiler. Arrange polenta slices on nonstick cookie sheet. In small bowl, mix Parmesan, thyme, 1/4 teaspoon salt, and 1/4 teaspoon pepper. Sprinkle 1 teaspoon cheese mixture on top of each polenta slice. Place cookie sheet in broiler at closest position to source of heat; broil polenta until cheese melts and top is golden, 6 to 8 minutes.

2. Meanwhile, in large bowl, with wire whisk, whisk vinegars, oil, mayonnaise, mustard, sugar, remaining 1/4 teaspoon salt, and 1/4 teaspoon pepper until blended. Add salad greens and toss until evenly coated.

3. To serve, divide salad greens among six salad plates. Top each salad with 3 warm polenta rounds.

Each serving: About 135 calories, 6 g protein, 14 g carbohydrate, 6 g total fat
(2 g saturated), 2 g fiber, 8 mg cholesterol, 630 mg sodium.

Lemon Broccoli

PREP 10 minutes   **STEAM** 5 minutes   **MAKES** 6 accompaniment servings

Ready-to-cook, precut broccoli flowerets are quickly steamed, then tossed with a savory lemon butter.

1	lemon	1/4	teaspoon salt
2	bags (12 ounces each) fresh broccoli flowerets	1/8	teaspoon ground black pepper
1	tablespoon butter or margarine		

1. From lemon, grate 1 teaspoon peel and squeeze 1 tablespoon juice; set aside.

2. Add about *3/4 inch water* to wide-bottomed 5- to 6-quart saucepot. Place collapsible steamer basket (about 11 inches in diameter) in saucepot; heat water to boiling over high heat. Add broccoli to steamer basket; cover and steam until broccoli is tender-crisp, 5 to 6 minutes.

3. In large serving bowl, toss broccoli with lemon peel and juice, butter, salt, and pepper.

Each serving: About 40 calories, 3 g protein, 5 g carbohydrate, 2 g total fat (0 g saturated), 3 g fiber, 0 mg cholesterol, 145 mg sodium.

Cajun Shrimp with Rémoulade Sauce

PREP 25 minutes   **GRILL** 4 minutes   **MAKES** 4 main-dish servings

This takes only four minutes on the fire! We added fresh lemon peel to jarred Cajun seasoning (a blend of garlic, onion, chiles, peppers, and herbs). The creamy homemade sauce pairs nicely with Southern-style shrimp.

Rémoulade Sauce
- 1/2 cup light mayonnaise
- 2 tablespoons ketchup
- 2 tablespoons minced celery
- 1 tablespoon Dijon mustard with seeds
- 1 tablespoon minced fresh parsley leaves
- 2 teaspoons fresh lemon juice
- 1/2 teaspoon Cajun seasoning*
- 1 green onion, minced

Cajun Shrimp
- 1 tablespoon Cajun seasoning*
- 1 tablespoon olive oil
- 2 teaspoons grated fresh lemon peel
- 1 1/4 pounds large shrimp, shelled and deveined, leaving tail part of shell on if you like
- lemon wedges (optional)

1. Prepare Rémoulade Sauce: In small bowl, mix mayonnaise, ketchup, celery, mustard, parsley, lemon juice, Cajun seasoning, and green onion. Cover and refrigerate up to 3 days if not serving right away. Makes about 1 cup.

2. Prepare charcoal fire or preheat gas grill for direct grilling over medium-high heat.

3. Prepare Cajun Shrimp: In medium bowl, mix Cajun seasoning, oil, and lemon peel. Add shrimp to spice mixture and toss until evenly coated.

4. Place shrimp on hot grill rack (or hot flat grill topper) and grill until shrimp are just opaque throughout, 3 to 4 minutes, turning once.

5. Transfer shrimp to platter; serve with lemon wedges, if you like, and Rémoulade Sauce.

Seasoning mixes vary among manufacturers, especially with regard to salt content. Add salt to taste if necessary.

Each serving shrimp: About 155 calories, 24 g protein, 2 g carbohydrate, 5 g total fat (1 g saturated), 0 g fiber, 175 mg cholesterol, 575 mg sodium.
Each 1 tablespoon sauce: About 30 calories, 0 g protein, 2 g carbohydrate, 3 g total fat (1 g saturated), 0 g fiber, 3 mg cholesterol, 95 mg sodium.

Braised Leeks

PREP 10 minutes **COOK** 15 minutes **MAKES** 4 accompaniment servings

1 **bunch leeks (1$1/2$ pounds)**	$1/8$ **teaspoon salt**
1 **tablespoon butter or margarine**	$1/4$ **cup water**

1. Cut off roots and trim dark green tops from leeks; cut each leek lengthwise in half, then crosswise into $1/2$-inch-thick slices. Rinse leeks in large bowl of cold water, swishing to remove sand; transfer to colander to drain, leaving sand in bottom of bowl.

2. In 2-quart saucepan, combine leeks, butter, salt, and water; heat to boiling over high heat. Reduce heat; cover and simmer until just tender, about 5 minutes. Remove cover; cook until water has evaporated, about 5 minutes longer.

Each serving: About 68 calories, 1 g protein, 10 g carbohydrate, 3 g total fat (2 g saturated), 3 g fiber, 8 mg cholesterol, 116 mg sodium.

Salmon Teriyaki

PREP 10 minutes **GRILL** 8 minutes **MAKES** 4 main-dish servings

6 tablespoons teriyaki sauce
1 tablespoon brown sugar
1 teaspoon Asian sesame oil
4 salmon steaks, 3/4 inch thick
  (6 ounces each)

1 green onion, thinly sliced on
  the diagonal

1. Prepare charcoal fire or preheat gas grill for covered direct grilling over medium heat.

2. Meanwhile, in 2-quart saucepan, heat teriyaki sauce, brown sugar, and sesame oil to boiling over medium-high heat. Boil until slightly thickened, 3 minutes.

3. Lightly oil salmon; place on hot rack. Cover and grill salmon, turning once and brushing frequently with teriyaki mixture, until salmon just turns opaque throughout, about 8 minutes.

4. Arrange salmon on platter; sprinkle with green onion.

Each serving: About 320 calories, 36 g protein, 8 g carbohydrate, 15 g total fat
(3 g saturated), 0 g fiber, 110 mg cholesterol, 1,120 mg sodium.

Grilled Portobello Mushroom Salad

PREP 20 minutes **GRILL** 9 minutes **MAKES** 4 first-course servings

Hearty portobellos are perfect for grilling. Baby greens make a good substitute for arugula.

1 **wedge Parmesan cheese**	1/4 **teaspoon salt**
2 **small bunches arugula (4 ounces each), trimmed**	1/8 **teaspoon ground black pepper**
2 **tablespoons balsamic vinegar**	1 **pound portobello mushrooms, stems removed**
2 **tablespoons olive oil**	
2 **tablespoons minced shallots**	
2 **tablespoons chopped fresh parsley**	

1. Prepare charcoal fire, preheat gas grill for direct grilling, or preheat broiler. With vegetable peeler, remove enough shavings from wedge of Parmesan to measure 1/2 cup, loosely packed (about 1 ounce). Arrange arugula on serving platter.

2. In small bowl, with wire whisk, mix vinegar, oil, shallots, parsley, salt, and pepper until blended. Place mushrooms, stem side down, on grill or on rack in broiling pan at closest position to heat source. Brush mushrooms with 1 tablespoon dressing. Grill or broil 4 minutes. Turn; brush mushrooms with 1 more tablespoon dressing. Grill or broil until tender, about 5 minutes longer.

3. Thinly slice mushrooms and arrange on arugula. Spoon remaining dressing over salad; top with Parmesan shavings.

Each serving: About 139 calories, 7 g protein, 9 g carbohydrate, 10 g total fat
(2 g saturated), 3 g fiber, 5 mg cholesterol, 285 mg sodium.

Salmon Steaks with Nectarine Salad

PREP 20 minutes **GRILL** 8 minutes **MAKES** 4 main-dish servings

1 tablespoon brown sugar
2 teaspoons vegetable oil
1 teaspoon ground coriander
1 1/2 teaspoons fresh thyme leaves
1 1/4 teaspoons salt
1/4 teaspoon coarsely ground pepper
4 salmon steaks, 3/4 inch thick (6 ounces each)
3 ripe nectarines (1 pound), pitted, each cut into quarters and thinly sliced crosswise

2 Kirby cucumbers (4 ounces each), each cut lengthwise in half, then thinly sliced crosswise
1 green onion, thinly sliced
1 tablespoon fresh lemon juice

1. Prepare charcoal fire or preheat gas grill for covered direct grilling over medium heat.

2. Meanwhile, in cup, combine brown sugar, oil, coriander, 1 teaspoon thyme, 3/4 teaspoon salt, and 1/8 teaspoon pepper. Use to rub on both sides of salmon steaks.

3. In medium bowl, stir nectarines, cucumbers, green onion, lemon juice, remaining 1/2 teaspoon thyme, 1/2 teaspoon salt, and 1/8 teaspoon pepper. Makes about 4 1/2 cups.

4. Lightly oil salmon; place on hot rack. Cover grill, and grill salmon until just opaque throughout, about 8 minutes, turning salmon once. Serve with Nectarine Salad.

Each serving: About 355 calories, 29 g protein, 18 g carbohydrate, 18 g total fat (3 g saturated), 2 g fiber, 80 mg cholesterol, 800 mg sodium.

Grilled Tuna on Spinach Salad

PREP 25 minutes   **COOK** 10 minutes   **MAKES** 4 main-dish servings

A blend of aromatic spices rubbed on tuna steaks before pan-grilling adds great flavor.

Tuna with Spice Rub
- 1 tablespoon olive oil
- 1 teaspoon ground cumin
- 1 teaspoon ground coriander
- 1 teaspoon paprika
- 1 teaspoon freshly grated lime peel
- 3/4 teaspoon salt
- 1/2 teaspoon coarsely ground black pepper
- 4 tuna or salmon steaks, 1 inch thick (6 ounces each)

Spinach Salad
- 2 tablespoons olive oil
- 2 tablespoons fresh lime juice
- 1 teaspoon sugar
- 1/4 teaspoon ground cumin
- 1/4 teaspoon salt
- 1/8 teaspoon coarsely ground black pepper
- 1 bag (6 ounces) baby spinach
- 1/2 English (seedless) cucumber (8 ounces), not peeled, cut lengthwise in half, then thinly sliced crosswise
- 1 bunch radishes, each cut in half, then thinly sliced

1. Prepare Spice Rub: In small bowl, with spoon, combine oil, cumin, coriander, paprika, lime peel, salt, and pepper until well blended.

2. Rub spice mixture on both sides of fish. Heat grill pan over medium heat until hot but not smoking. Add fish to pan and cook, until fish just turns opaque throughout, 8 to 10 minutes, turning fish once. Transfer fish to cutting board.

3. Meanwhile, prepare Spinach Salad: In large bowl, with wire whisk, mix oil, lime juice, sugar, cumin, salt, and pepper until dressing is blended. Add spinach, cucumber, and sliced radishes; toss to coat.

4. Cut fish into 1/2-inch-thick slices. Arrange Spinach Salad on four dinner plates or large platter; top with fish.

Each serving: About 300 calories, 42 g protein, 5 g carbohydrate, 12 g total fat
(2 g saturated), 5 g fiber, 76 mg cholesterol, 700 mg sodium.

Asian Flounder Bake

PREP 5 minutes   **BAKE** 12 minutes   **MAKES** 4 main-dish servings

1/4 cup reduced-sodium soy sauce
2   tablespoons dry sherry
1   teaspoon sugar
1   teaspoon grated peeled fresh
    ginger
1   teaspoon Asian sesame oil
1   bag (10 ounces) shredded
    carrots

1   bag (5 to 6 ounces) baby
    spinach
4   flounder or sole fillets
    (5 ounces each)
1   green onion, thinly sliced
1   tablespoon sesame seeds,
    toasted (optional)

1. Preheat oven to 450°F. In 1-cup liquid measuring cup, combine soy sauce, sherry, sugar, ginger, and sesame oil.

2. In bottom of 13" by 9" baking dish, spread carrots evenly. Place spinach over carrots, then top with flounder. Pour soy-sauce mixture evenly over flounder.

3. Bake until fish turns opaque throughout, 12 to 14 minutes. To serve, sprinkle with green onion and top with sesame seeds, if using.

Each serving: About 200 calories, 30 g protein, 11 g carbohydrate, 3 g total fat (1 g saturated), 6 g fiber, 68 mg cholesterol, 735 mg sodium.

Stir-Fried Bok Choy

PREP 10 minutes   **COOK** 10 minutes   **MAKES** 4 accompaniment servings

This is the classic Chinese preparation, and it is as delicious as it is simple.

1   head bok choy (2 pounds)
1   tablespoon vegetable oil

1   garlic clove, crushed with side
    of chef's knife
2   tablespoons soy sauce

1. Cut bok choy stalks from leaves; cut stalks and leaves, separately, into 1/2-inch-thick slices.

2. In 10-inch skillet, heat oil over medium-high heat. Add garlic and cook until golden. Add bok choy stalks and cook, stirring frequently (stir-frying) until just tender, about 4 minutes. Add bok choy leaves and stir-fry until wilted, about 2 minutes longer. Stir in soy sauce and remove from heat.

Each serving: About 62 calories, 3 g protein, 5 g carbohydrate, 4 g total fat
(0 g saturated), 5 g fiber, 0 mg cholesterol, 644 mg sodium.

Shrimp and Tomato Summer Salad

PREP 25 minutes   **MAKES** 6 main-dish servings

2 tablespoons olive oil
2 tablespoons red wine vinegar
3/4 teaspoon salt
1/4 teaspoon coarsely ground black pepper
1/2 cup loosely packed fresh parsley leaves, chopped
1/4 cup loosely packed fresh mint leaves, thinly sliced
1 pound shelled and deveined cooked large shrimp

2 1/2 pounds ripe tomatoes (4 large), cut into 1-inch pieces
1 English (seedless) cucumber or 4 Kirby cucumbers, cut lengthwise into quarters, then cut crosswise into 1-inch pieces
1 small red onion, chopped
2 ounces feta cheese, crumbled (about 1/2 cup)

1. In serving bowl, with wire whisk, whisk together oil, vinegar, salt, and pepper; stir in parsley and mint.

2. Add shrimp, tomatoes, cucumber, and onion to dressing in bowl; stir to combine. Sprinkle salad with feta to serve. Serve at room temperature or cover and refrigerate to serve later.

Each serving: About 200 calories, 20 g protein, 13 g carbohydrate, 8 g total fat (2 g saturated), 3 g fiber, 156 mg cholesterol, 585 mg sodium.

Mussels with Capers and White Wine

PREP 15 minutes   **BAKE** 10 minutes   **MAKES** 4 main-dish servings

Shellfish steamed with garlic, capers, and wine make a dinner that can be ready in minutes.

1 tablespoon butter or margarine	2 tablespoons drained capers
1 medium shallot, finely chopped (2 tablespoons)	3 pounds mussels, scrubbed and debearded
2 garlic cloves, crushed with garlic press	1/2 cup loosely packed fresh parsley leaves, chopped
1/2 cup dry white wine	

1. In 5- to 6-quart saucepot or Dutch oven, melt butter over medium-high heat. Add shallot and garlic and cook, stirring frequently, 2 minutes. Stir in wine and capers and heat to boiling; boil 2 minutes.

2. Add mussels to saucepot; reduce heat. Cover and simmer 10 minutes until shells open, transferring mussels to bowl as they open. Discard any mussels that have not opened.

3. Serve mussels in bowls with sauce. Sprinkle with parsley.

Each serving: About 201 calories, 21 g protein, 9 g carbohydrate, 7 g total fat (3 g saturated), 0 g fiber, 55 mg cholesterol, 650 mg sodium.

Mixed Pea Pod Stir-Fry

PREP 15 minutes   **COOK** 16 minutes   **MAKES** 4 accompaniment servings

This sweet and tender-crisp medley celebrates the glorious flavor of fresh green vegetables.

1 teaspoon salt	4 ounces sugar snap peas, trimmed and strings removed
8 ounces green beans, trimmed	
2 teaspoons vegetable oil	1 garlic clove, finely chopped
4 ounces snow peas, trimmed and strings removed	1 tablespoon soy sauce

1. In 12-inch skillet, combine *4 cups water* and salt; heat to boiling over high heat. Add green beans and cook 3 minutes. Drain; wipe skillet dry with paper towels.

2. In same skillet, heat oil over high heat. Add green beans and cook, stirring frequently (stir-frying), until they begin to brown, 2 to 3 minutes. Add snow peas, sugar snap peas, and garlic; stir-fry until snow peas and sugar snap peas are tender-crisp, about 1 minute longer. Stir in soy sauce and remove from heat.

Each serving: About 63 calories, 3 g protein, 8 g carbohydrate, 2 g total fat (0 g saturated), 4 g fiber, 0 mg cholesterol, 844 mg sodium.

Vegetables, Eggs, and Cheese

Herb and Feta Frittata

PREP 10 minutes   **COOK** 20 minutes   **MAKES** 4 main-dish servings

This easy one-dish supper is a great jumping-off point for many variations: Try adding two cups of packed leafy greens like baby spinach or arugula to the hot oil in the skillet; cook just until wilted before adding egg mixture. Or experiment with different varieties of cheese, such as half-inch chunks of Brie, shredded Gruyère, or crumbled goat cheese.

2 teaspoons olive oil	1/4 cup whole milk
8 large eggs	2 tablespoons fresh rosemary
4 ounces feta cheese, crumbled (1 cup)	or thyme leaves, chopped
1/3 cup loosely packed fresh parsley or basil leaves, chopped	1/2 teaspoon ground black pepper

1. Preheat oven to 400°F. In nonstick 10-inch skillet with oven-safe handle (if skillet is not oven-safe, wrap handle with double layer of foil), heat oil over medium heat until hot.

2. Meanwhile, in medium bowl with wire whisk, whisk eggs, feta, parsley, milk, rosemary, and pepper until blended. Pour egg mixture into skillet; do not stir. Cook until egg mixture begins to set around edge, 3 to 4 minutes.

3. Place skillet in oven; bake until frittata is set, 13 to 15 minutes. Cut frittata into wedges to serve.

Each serving: About 255 calories, 17 g protein, 4 g carbohydrate, 19 g total fat (8 g saturated), 0 g fiber, 452 mg cholesterol, 450 mg sodium.

Scrambled Eggs with Chives

PREP 10 minutes   **COOK** 10 minutes   **MAKES** 12 main-dish servings

Here's an easy meal for a crowd: Fluffy eggs spiked with chives alongside savory biscuits topped with sesame seeds. Add Roasted-Prosciutto Wrapped Asparagus (page 193) and you can feed the whole gang!

24 **large eggs**
3/4 **cup low-fat (1%) milk**
1/2 **cup snipped fresh chives**
    (2 large bunches)
3/4 **teaspoon salt**

1/4 **teaspoon coarsely ground**
    black pepper
2 **tablespoons butter or**
    margarine

1. In large bowl, with wire whisk, beat eggs, milk, chives, salt, and pepper until blended.

2. In deep nonstick 12-inch skillet, melt butter over medium-high heat. Add egg mixture to skillet. As egg mixture begins to set around edge, stir lightly with heat-safe rubber spatula or wooden spoon to allow uncooked egg mixture to flow toward side of pan. Continue cooking until eggs are set to desired doneness, 7 to 10 minutes.

Each serving: About 175 calories, 13 g protein, 2 g carbohydrate, 12 g total fat (5 g saturated), 0 g fiber, 435 mg cholesterol, 296 mg sodium.

Benne Biscuits

PREP 15 minutes **BAKE** 12 minutes **MAKES** 16 biscuits

Tender buttermilk biscuits are glazed with egg white and sprinkled with benne seeds—the Southern term for sesame seeds.

3 cups cake flour (not self-rising)	1 large egg white
2¹/4 teaspoons baking powder	1¹/4 cups buttermilk
³/4 teaspoon baking soda	4 teaspoons benne (sesame) seeds
³/4 teaspoon salt	
6 tablespoons vegetable shortening	

1. Preheat oven to 450°F. Into large bowl, measure cake flour, baking powder, baking soda, and salt; stir until combined. With pastry blender or 2 knives used scissor-fashion, cut in shortening until fine crumbs form. In cup, with fork, beat egg white with *1 teaspoon water*; set aside.

2. Add buttermilk to flour mixture; stir just until dough is evenly moistened. (For tender biscuits, do not overmix.)

3. On lightly floured surface, pat dough into 7-inch square. Cut dough into 4 strips, then cut each strip crosswise into 4 pieces to make 16 biscuits. Brush biscuits with egg white and sprinkle with seeds.

4. Place biscuits on ungreased large cookie sheet. Bake biscuits until lightly golden, 12 to 15 minutes. Serve biscuits warm, or cool on wire rack to serve later. Reheat before serving if you like.

Each biscuit: About 130 calories, 3 g protein, 17 g carbohydrate, 6 g total fat (1 g saturated), 0 g fiber, 1 mg cholesterol, 250 mg sodium.

Roasted Prosciutto-Wrapped Asparagus

PREP 30 minutes   **STEAM/ROAST** 20 minutes   **MAKES** 12 first-course servings

You can oven-steam the asparagus in advance, then roast the wrapped spears just before serving. The recipe works best with medium-size asparagus spears because they're easier to handle as finger food.

24   medium asparagus spears
     (1¹/2 pounds), trimmed
12   thin slices prosciutto (8
     ounces), each cut lengthwise
     in half
¹/2 cup grated Parmesan cheese

1. Preheat oven to 400°F. Place asparagus and *1/4 cup boiling water* in large roasting pan (17" by 11¹/2"); cover pan with foil. Steam asparagus until tender when tested with tip of knife, 10 to 15 minutes. Transfer asparagus to paper towels to drain. Wipe pan dry.

2. On sheet of waxed paper, place 1 strip prosciutto; sprinkle with 1 teaspoon Parmesan. Place asparagus spear on 1 end of prosciutto strip. Roll prosciutto around asparagus spear, slightly overlapping prosciutto as you roll, and covering most of spear. Repeat with remaining asparagus, prosciutto, and Parmesan.

3. Place wrapped asparagus in roasting pan (it's alright if spears touch), and roast until asparagus is heated through and prosciutto just begins to brown, 10 minutes.

Each serving: About 50 calories, 7 g protein, 1 g carbohydrate,
2 g total fat (1 g saturated), 1 g fiber, 15 mg cholesterol, 540 mg sodium.

VARIATION

Black Forest Ham–Wrapped Asparagus: Substitute *12 thin slices Black Forest ham* (about 8 ounces) for prosciutto and use *1 cup shredded Gruyère cheese* (about 1¹/2 teaspoons per spear) for Parmesan. Follow recipe as above.

Each serving: About 80 calories, 8 g protein, 1 g carbohydrate, 5 g total fat (2 g saturated),
1 g fiber, 21 mg cholesterol, 315 mg sodium.

Eggs Florentine

PREP 25 minutes **BAKE** 20 minutes **MAKES** 6 main-dish servings

1 log (16 ounces) precooked polenta	pinch ground red pepper (cayenne)
6 slices Canadian-style bacon (4 ounces)	1 package (10 ounces) frozen chopped spinach, thawed and squeezed dry
1 1/2 cups low-fat (1%) milk	
1 tablespoon cornstarch	1/4 cup grated Parmesan cheese
1/2 teaspoon salt	6 large eggs

1. Preheat oven to 400°F. Grease shallow 2 1/2-quart casserole. Cut polenta log in half, then cut each half lengthwise into 3 long slices. Place polenta slices in single layer in casserole. Bake polenta slices until heated through, 15 minutes. Top each polenta slice with 1 slice bacon; return to oven and bake 5 minutes longer. Keep warm.

2. Meanwhile, in 2-quart saucepan, with wire whisk, mix milk, cornstarch, salt, ground red pepper, and *1/2 cup water* until blended. Cook over medium-high heat until mixture thickens and boils; boil 1 minute, stirring. Stir in spinach and Parmesan; heat through.

3. Poach eggs: In 12-inch skillet, heat *1 1/2 inches water* to boiling over medium-high heat. Reduce heat to medium to maintain water at a gentle simmer. Break cold eggs, 1 at a time, into cup; holding cup close to surface of water, slip in each egg. Cook eggs 3 to 5 minutes. With slotted spoon, lift out each egg; quickly drain in spoon on paper towels.

4. To serve, place a bacon-topped polenta slice on each of 6 plates. Spoon spinach mixture over bacon and polenta; top each with a poached egg.

Each serving: About 215 calories, 16 g protein, 18 g carbohydrate, 8 g total fat (3 g saturated), 2 g fiber, 226 mg cholesterol, 995 mg sodium.

SERVING SUGGESTION
A mixed green salad with balsamic vinaigrette.

Spring Onion, Spinach, and Pecorino Frittata

PREP 10 minutes   **COOK** 20 minutes   **MAKES** 4 main-dish servings

2	spring onions (12 ounces, with tops) or 1 large sweet onion	8	large eggs
2	teaspoons olive oil	1/4	cup grated Pecorino-Romano cheese
1	bag (5 to 6 ounces) baby spinach	1/2	teaspoon salt
		1/4	teaspoon coarsely ground black pepper

1. Preheat oven to 425°F. Trim tough green leaves from top of spring onions. Cut stems crosswise into 1/4-inch-thick slices. Cut each onion bulb in half and thinly slice.

2. In nonstick 12-inch skillet with oven-safe handle (if skillet is not oven-safe, wrap handle with double layer of foil), heat oil over medium heat until hot. Add sliced onions and stems and cook, stirring occasionally, until soft and golden brown, 10 minutes. Stir in spinach and cook, stirring constantly, just until wilted, 1 minute. Spread onion mixture evenly in skillet; remove skillet from heat.

3. In medium bowl, with wire whisk, whisk eggs, Pecorino, *1/4 cup water*, salt, and pepper until blended.

4. Carefully pour the egg mixture into skillet over the onion mixture; do not stir. Return to medium-high heat and cook until egg mixture begins to set around the edge, 2 to 3 minutes.

5. Place skillet in oven; bake until frittata is set, 8 to 10 minutes. Slide out of skillet onto cutting board. Cut into wedges to serve.

Each serving: About 215 calories, 16 g protein, 7 g carbohydrate, 14 g total fat (4 g saturated), 5 g fiber, 430 mg cholesterol, 530 mg sodium.

SERVING SUGGESTION
Warmed whole-wheat pita bread and sweet or hot Italian sausages.

Asparagus and Green-Onion Frittata

PREP 25 minutes   **COOK** 10 minutes   **MAKES** 4 main-dish servings

Everyone loves a skillet omelet, especially when it's filled with bits of cream cheese and sautéed vegetables.

8 large eggs	1 tablespoon butter or margarine
1/2 cup whole milk	
1/8 teaspoon ground black pepper	1 bunch green onions, chopped
3/4 teaspoon salt	2 ounces light cream cheese (Neufchâtel)
12 ounces asparagus, trimmed	

1. Preheat oven to 375°F. In medium bowl, with wire whisk, beat eggs, milk, pepper, and 1/2 teaspoon salt until blended; set aside. If using thin asparagus, cut each stalk crosswise in half; if using medium asparagus, cut stalks into 1-inch pieces.

2. In nonstick 10-inch skillet with oven-safe handle (if skillet is not oven-safe, wrap handle with double layer of foil), melt butter over medium heat. Add asparagus and remaining 1/4 teaspoon salt; cook 4 minutes for thin stalks or 6 minutes for medium-size stalks, stirring often. Stir in green onions and cook, stirring occasionally, until vegetables are tender, 2 to 3 minutes longer.

3. Reduce heat to medium-low. Pour egg mixture over vegetables in skillet; drop scant teaspoonfuls of cream cheese on top of egg mixture. Cook, without stirring, until egg mixture begins to set around edge, 3 to 4 minutes. Place skillet in oven and bake until frittata is set, 10 to 12 minutes. Cut into wedges to serve.

Each serving: About 251 calories, 17 g protein, 6 g carbohydrate, 18 g total fat (8 g saturated), 1 g fiber, 448 mg cholesterol, 689 mg sodium.

Egg Salad Deluxe

PREP 20 minutes **COOK** 20 minutes **MAKES** about 4¹/₂ cups or 6 main-dish servings

Hard-cooked eggs are chopped and mixed with sautéed onions, mushrooms, and celery for a new take on the classic egg salad.

8 large eggs	¹/₄ cup loosely packed fresh parsley leaves, chopped
3 tablespoons olive oil	
1 medium onion, cut in half and thinly sliced	¹/₂ teaspoon salt
	¹/₄ teaspoon coarsely ground black pepper
10 ounces mushrooms, sliced	
2 medium celery stalks, finely chopped	1 head Boston lettuce, leaves separated

1. In 3-quart saucepan, place eggs and enough *cold water* to cover by at least 1 inch; heat to boiling over high heat. Immediately remove saucepan from heat and cover tightly; let stand 15 minutes. Cool eggs under cold running water until easy to handle.

2. Meanwhile, in nonstick 12-inch skillet, heat 1 tablespoon oil over medium heat until hot. Add onion and cook, stirring occasionally, until tender and golden, 10 to 12 minutes. Increase heat to medium-high; add mushrooms and cook until mushrooms are golden and all liquid evaporates, 8 minutes.

3. Remove shells from hard-cooked eggs. Finely chop eggs. In large bowl, toss eggs with mushroom mixture, celery, parsley, salt, pepper, and remaining 2 tablespoons oil.

4. To serve, line platter with lettuce leaves and top with egg salad.

Each serving: About 190 calories, 11 g protein, 5 g carbohydrate, 14 g total fat (3 g saturated), 1 g fiber, 283 mg cholesterol, 290 mg sodium.

Roasted Asparagus

PREP 10 minutes   **ROAST** 20 minutes   **MAKES** 6 accompaniment servings

Roasting is a no-fuss way to cook asparagus—and it brings out the natural sweet flavor of the vegetable.

2 **pounds asparagus, trimmed**	**1/4** **teaspoon salt**
1 **tablespoon olive oil**	**1/4** **teaspoon ground black pepper**

1. Preheat oven to 400°F. In broiling pan without rack or in large roasting pan (17" by 11 1/2"), toss asparagus with oil, salt, and pepper.

2. Roast asparagus until tender and lightly browned, 15 to 20 minutes.

Each serving: About 45 calories, 3 g protein, 2 g carbohydrate, 3 g total fat (0 g saturated), 1 g fiber, 0 mg cholesterol, 110 mg sodium.

Grilled Tofu and Veggies

PREP 25 minutes   **GRILL** 12 minutes   **MAKES** 4 main-dish servings

Go beyond veggie burgers. Shake things up for nonmeat eaters with a barbecue surprise: tender tofu, zucchini, and pepper with a great hoisin-ginger glaze. Be sure to buy extrafirm tofu; other varieties will fall apart while cooking.

Hoisin Glaze
- 1/3 cup hoisin sauce
- 2 garlic cloves, crushed with garlic press
- 1 tablespoon vegetable oil
- 1 tablespoon reduced-sodium soy sauce
- 1 tablespoon grated, peeled fresh ginger
- 1 tablespoon seasoned rice vinegar
- 1/8 teaspoon ground red pepper (cayenne)

Tofu and Veggies
- 1 package (15 ounces) extrafirm tofu
- 2 medium zucchini (10 ounces each), each cut lengthwise into quarters, then crosswise in half
- 1 large red pepper, cut lengthwise into quarters, stem and seeds discarded
- 1 bunch green onions, trimmed
- 1 teaspoon vegetable oil

1. Prepare charcoal fire or preheat gas grill for direct grilling over medium heat.

2. Prepare Hoisin Glaze: In small bowl, with fork, mix hoisin, garlic, oil, soy sauce, ginger, vinegar, and ground red pepper until well blended.

3. Prepare Tofu and Veggies: Cut tofu horizontally into 4 pieces, then cut each piece crosswise in half. Place tofu on paper towels; pat dry with additional paper towels. Spoon half of Hoisin Glaze into medium bowl; add zucchini and red pepper. Gently toss vegetables to coat with glaze. Arrange tofu on large plate, and brush both sides of tofu with remaining glaze. On another plate, rub green onions with oil.

4. Place tofu, zucchini, and red pepper on hot grill rack. Grill tofu 6 minutes, gently turning over once with wide metal spatula. Transfer tofu to platter; keep warm. Continue grilling vegetables until tender and browned,

about 5 minutes longer, removing them to platter with tofu as they are done. Add green onions to grill during last minute of cooking time, and grill until lightly browned; transfer to platter.

Each serving: About 245 calories, 15 g protein, 22 g carbohydrate, 11 g total fat (1 g saturated), 4 g fiber, 0 mg cholesterol, 615 mg sodium.

Smart Carbs

Spinach Salad with Warm Bacon Dressing

PREP 5 minutes   **COOK** 10 minutes   **MAKES** 4 main-dish serving

Cut hours off the prep time for this filling main-dish salad by buying already roasted and sliced chicken breast to toss with a homemade warm-from-the-skillet dressing.

6 slices bacon (4 ounces)	1 can (11 ounces) mandarin-orange segments, drained
1/4 cup cider vinegar	
2 tablespoons olive oil	1 package (10 ounces) carved cooked chicken breast
1 tablespoon sugar	
2 teaspoons Dijon mustard	1 bag (6 to 7 ounces) baby spinach
1/4 teaspoon ground black pepper	

1. In 10-inch skillet, cook bacon over medium heat until browned, 8 minutes, turning once. Transfer bacon to paper towels to drain. Discard all but 1 tablespoon bacon drippings from skillet.

2. Into drippings in skillet, stir vinegar, oil, sugar, mustard, and pepper until blended. Heat dressing over medium-low heat 1 minute.

3. In large bowl, toss orange segments, chicken, and spinach with warm dressing until salad is evenly coated. Crumble bacon over salad.

Each serving: About 275 calories, 24 g protein, 10 g carbohydrate, 17 g total fat (4 g saturated), 5 g fiber, 61 mg cholesterol, 725 mg sodium.

SERVING SUGGESTION
Warmed whole-wheat pita bread.

Vegetarian Phyllo Pizza

PREP 10 minutes **BAKE** 15 minutes **MAKES** 4 main-dish servings

This interesting take on the Italian pie is on the table in less than thirty minutes. For a kid-friendly version, substitute shredded mozzarella and sliced pepperoni for the goat cheese and artichokes. This pizza also makes great appetizers—cut into bite-size pieces to serve.

6 sheets (17" by 12" each) fresh or frozen (thawed) phyllo	1 jar (6 ounces) marinated artichoke hearts, drained and cut into cubes
2 tablespoons butter or margarine, melted	1 1/2 cups grape or cherry tomatoes, each cut in half
4 ounces soft, mild goat cheese such as Montrachet	

1. Preheat oven to 450°F. Place 1 sheet of phyllo on ungreased large cookie sheet; brush with some melted butter. Repeat layering with remaining phyllo and butter; do not brush top layer.

2. Crumble goat cheese over phyllo; top with artichokes and tomatoes. Bake pizza until golden brown around the edges, 12 to 15 minutes.

3. Transfer pizza to large cutting board. With pizza cutter or knife, cut pizza lengthwise in half, then cut each half crosswise into 4 pieces.

Each serving: About 247 calories, 8 g protein, 20 g carbohydrate, 16 g total fat (9 g saturated), 2 g fiber, 29 mg cholesterol, 423 mg sodium.

Tomato and Cheese Pie

PREP 20 minutes **BAKE** 30 minutes **MAKES** 6 main-dish servings

A savory custard pie that bakes right in the pie plate—with no crust!

1   container (15 ounces)
    part-skim ricotta cheese
4   large eggs
1/4 cup grated Parmesan cheese
3/4 teaspoon salt plus additional
    for sprinkling
1/8 teaspoon coarsely ground
    black pepper plus additional
    for sprinkling

1/4 cup low-fat (1%) milk
1   tablespoon cornstarch
1   cup packed fresh basil leaves,
    chopped
1   pound ripe tomatoes
    (3 medium), thinly sliced

1. Preheat oven to 375°F. In large bowl, with wire whisk, beat ricotta, eggs, Parmesan, salt, and pepper until blended.

2. In cup, stir milk and cornstarch until smooth; whisk into cheese mixture. Stir in basil.

3. Pour mixture into 9-inch pie plate. Arrange tomatoes on top, overlapping if necessary. Sprinkle tomatoes with salt and pepper. Bake pie until lightly browned around edge and center is puffed, 30 to 35 minutes.

Each serving: About 190 calories, 15 g protein, 10 g carbohydrate, 10 g total fat
(5 g saturated), 1 g fiber, 167 mg cholesterol, 515 mg sodium.

Mixed Summer Squash with Parsley and Lemon

PREP 15 minutes   **COOK** 5 minutes   **MAKES** 6 accompaniment servings

4	small zucchini and/or yellow summer squash (6 ounces each)	1/4	teaspoon coarsely ground pepper
1	tablespoon butter or margarine	1/4	cup loosely packed fresh parsley leaves, chopped
1/2	teaspoon salt	1/2	teaspoon grated fresh lemon peel

1. Cut squash diagonally into 1/4-inch-wide slices; then cut slices crosswise into 1/4-inch-wide strips.

2. In nonstick 12-inch skillet, melt butter over medium-high heat. Add squash, salt, and pepper; cook, stirring frequently, until squash is tender-crisp, 4 to 5 minutes. Stir in parsley and lemon peel.

Each serving: About 40 calories, 1 g protein, 5 g carbohydrate, 2 g total fat (1 g saturated), 2 g fiber, 5 mg cholesterol, 214 mg sodium.

Hot and Sour Soup

PREP 15 minutes   **COOK** 15 minutes   **MAKES** about 8 cups or 4 main-dish servings

We streamlined seasonings to help get this popular Asian soup on the table in record time—without sacrificing the great taste.

1	tablespoon vegetable oil
4	ounces shiitake mushrooms, stems discarded, caps thinly sliced
3	tablespoons reduced-sodium soy sauce
1	package (15 ounces) extrafirm tofu, drained, patted dry, and cut into 1-inch cubes
2	tablespoons cornstarch
1	container (32 ounces) chicken broth (4 cups)

3	tablespoons seasoned rice vinegar
2	tablespoons grated, peeled fresh ginger
1	tablespoon Worcestershire sauce
1/2	teaspoon Asian sesame oil
1/4	teaspoon ground red pepper (cayenne)
2	large eggs, beaten
2	green onions, sliced

1. In nonstick 5-quart saucepot, heat vegetable oil over medium-high heat until hot. Add mushrooms, soy sauce, and tofu; cook, gently stirring often, until liquid evaporates, 5 minutes.

2. In cup, with fork, mix cornstarch with *1/4 cup water*; set aside. Add broth and *3/4 cup water* to tofu mixture; heat to boiling. Stir in cornstarch mixture and boil 30 seconds, stirring. Reduce heat to medium-low; add vinegar, ginger, Worcestershire, sesame oil, and ground red pepper; simmer 5 minutes.

3. Remove saucepot from heat. Slowly pour beaten eggs into soup in a thin, steady stream around the edge of the saucepot. Carefully stir the soup once in a circular motion so egg separates into strands. Sprinkle with green onions.

Each serving: About 280 calories, 18 g protein, 17 g carbohydrate, 15 g total fat (3 g saturated), 1 g fiber, 106 mg cholesterol, 1,790 mg sodium.

Thai Coconut Soup

PREP 10 minutes   **COOK** 10 minutes   **MAKES** about 9 cups or 4 main-dish servings

2   small carrots, each cut crosswise in half
1/2   medium red pepper
1   can (14 ounces) light unsweetened coconut milk (not cream of coconut), well stirred
2   garlic cloves, crushed with garlic press
1   two-inch piece peeled fresh ginger, cut into 4 slices
1/2   teaspoon ground coriander
1/2   teaspoon ground cumin

1/4   teaspoon ground red pepper (cayenne)
12   ounces firm tofu, cut into 1-inch cubes
2   cans (14 1/2 ounces each) vegetable broth or chicken broth
1   tablespoon Asian fish sauce
1   tablespoon fresh lime juice
2   green onions, sliced
1/2   cup chopped fresh cilantro leaves

1. With vegetable peeler, remove lengthwise strips from carrots and edge of red pepper. Set aside.

2. In 5-quart Dutch oven, heat 1/2 cup coconut milk to boiling over medium heat. Add garlic, ginger, coriander, cumin, and ground red pepper; cook, stirring, 1 minute.

3. Increase heat to medium-high. Stir in carrot strips, pepper strips, tofu, broth, fish sauce, lime juice, *1 cup water*, and remaining coconut milk; heat just to simmering. Discard ginger. Stir in green onions and cilantro just before serving.

Each serving: About 210 calories, 11 g protein, 14 g carbohydrate, 17 g total fat (6 g saturated), 2 g fiber, 0 mg cholesterol, 1,060 mg sodium.

SERVING SUGGESTION
A watercress and endive salad with grapefruit segments.

Roasted Eggplant Parmesan

PREP 35 minutes   **ROAST/COOK** 45 minutes   **MAKES** 6 main-dish servings

Eggplant Parmesan usually requires lots of frying—but not our streamlined recipe.

2 small eggplants (1¼ pounds each), cut into ½-inch-thick slices	¼ teaspoon ground black pepper
¼ cup olive oil	⅓ cup chopped fresh parsley
½ teaspoon salt	4 ounces mozzarella cheese, shredded (1 cup)
1 can (28 ounces) plum tomatoes, drained and chopped	½ cup freshly grated Parmesan cheese

1. Preheat oven to 450°F. Place eggplant on two large cookie sheets. Brush oil on both sides of eggplant and sprinkle with ¼ teaspoon salt. Roast 15 minutes; turn slices and roast until eggplant has browned and is tender, 20 to 25 minutes.

2. Meanwhile, in nonstick 12-inch skillet, combine tomatoes, remaining ¼ teaspoon salt, and pepper; cook over low heat, stirring occasionally, until tomatoes have thickened, about 20 minutes. Stir in parsley.

3. Turn oven control to 400°F. In shallow 2½-quart casserole, layer half of eggplant and top with half of tomato sauce; sprinkle with half of mozzarella. Repeat layers; top with grated Parmesan.

4. Cover loosely with foil. Bake until bubbling, about 10 minutes. Remove casserole from oven and let stand at least 10 minutes before serving. Serve hot or at room temperature.

Each serving: About 248 calories, 11 g protein, 19 g carbohydrate, 16 g total fat (5 g saturated), 6 g fiber, 21 mg cholesterol, 693 mg sodium.

Skillet Cherry Tomatoes

PREP 5 minutes **COOK** 3 minutes **MAKES** 4 accompaniment servings

From start to finish, this cherry tomato side dish takes little more than five minutes.

1 **tablespoon butter or margarine**	1/8 **teaspoon salt**
1 **pint ripe cherry tomatoes**	**chopped parsley**

In 10-inch skillet, melt butter over medium-high heat. Add cherry tomatoes and salt and cook, shaking skillet frequently, just until heated through and skins split, about 2 minutes. Sprinkle with parsley.

Each serving: About 36 calories, 0 g protein, 2 g carbohydrate, 3 g total fat (2 g saturated), 1 g fiber, 8 mg cholesterol, 107 mg sodium.

Smart Carbs

Basic Fluffy Omelet

PREP 10 minutes **COOK/BAKE** 15 minutes **MAKES** 2 main-dish servings

Beaten egg whites give this oven-baked omelet extra lift. For a cheese omelet, sprinkle with your favorite shredded cheese during the last minute of baking.

4 **large eggs, separated**	1/8 **teaspoon salt**
2 **tablespoons water**	1 **tablespoon butter or margarine**

1. Preheat oven to 350°F. In medium bowl, with mixer at high speed, beat egg whites until stiff peaks form when beaters are lifted. In large bowl, with mixer at high speed, beat egg yolks, water, and salt until egg-yolk mixture has thickened. With rubber spatula, gently fold one-third of beaten egg whites into egg-yolk mixture. Fold in remaining egg whites until just blended.

2. In oven-safe nonstick 10-inch skillet (if skillet is not oven-safe, wrap handle with double layer of foil), melt butter over medium-low heat. Add

egg mixture and cook until top has puffed and underside is golden, about 3 minutes.

3. Place skillet in oven. Bake until top of omelet is golden and center springs back when lightly touched with finger, about 10 minutes.

4. To serve, loosen omelet from skillet and slide onto warm platter.

Each serving: About 200 calories, 13 g protein, 1 g carbohydrate, 16 g total fat (7 g saturated), 0 g fiber, 441 mg cholesterol, 331 mg sodium.

SERVING SUGGESTION
Whole-wheat toast wedges.

QUICK NO-COOK FILLINGS FOR OMELETS
In the mood for a deliciously different omelet? Try one of these flavorful combinations.
- **Mango chutney and sour cream**
- **Diced avocado, salsa, and sour cream**
- **Chopped tomato and pesto**
- **Chopped smoked salmon, cubed cream cheese, and capers**
- **Chopped smoked turkey, thinly sliced red onion, and cubed Brie cheese**
- **Chopped tomato, crumbled feta cheese, and dill**
- **Diced ham, chopped green onions, and shredded Pepper Jack cheese**
- **Caponata and grated Parmesan cheese**
- **Ricotta cheese, berries, and confectioners' sugar**
- **Crumbled goat cheese, jalapeño jelly, and sour cream**
- **Chopped fresh herbs, green onions, and sour cream**

Spinach Roulade with Mushrooms

PREP 25 minutes   **BAKE** 15 minutes   **MAKES** 8 main-dish servings

Spinach gives this roll its attractive green color.

1 tablespoon butter or margarine	1 package (10 ounces) frozen chopped spinach, thawed and squeezed dry
2 green onions, thinly sliced	
8 ounces white mushrooms, trimmed and coarsely chopped	6 large eggs
8 ounces shiitake mushrooms, stems removed and caps thinly sliced	2/3 cup milk
	1/2 cup freshly grated Parmesan cheese
1/2 teaspoon salt	6 ounces mild or sharp Cheddar cheese, shredded (1 1/2 cups)
1/4 teaspoon ground black pepper	

1. Preheat oven to 350°F. Line 15 1/2" by 10 1/2" jelly-roll pan with foil, leaving 2-inch overhang at each short end; grease foil.

2. In nonstick 12-inch skillet, melt butter over medium heat. Add green onions and cook until wilted, about 1 minute. Add white and shiitake mushrooms, salt, and pepper; cook, stirring frequently, until mushrooms are tender and liquid has evaporated, about 7 minutes. Remove from heat.

3. In blender, puree spinach, eggs, milk, and Parmesan until smooth. Pour into prepared pan, smoothing top with rubber spatula. Bake just until spinach mixture is set, 8 to 10 minutes. Lift foil with spinach mixture and place on surface. Sprinkle with Cheddar and spread mushroom mixture on top. Roll up from one long end, using foil to help roll and place, seam side down, in jelly-roll pan. Bake until Cheddar melts, about 5 minutes longer. To serve, using serrated knife, cut into 8 thick slices.

Each serving: About 217 calories, 15 g protein, 6 g carbohydrate, 15 g total fat (8 g saturated), 2 g fiber, 193 mg cholesterol, 490 mg sodium.

SERVING SUGGESTION
Sautéed cherry tomatoes.

Tofu "Egg Salad"

PREP 15 minutes   **MAKES** 4 main-dish servings

The familiar egg-salad seasonings lend themselves well to tofu.

1 **package (16 ounces) firm tofu, drained**	1 **green onion, chopped**
1 **stalk celery, chopped**	1/4 **cup low-fat mayonnaise dressing**
1/2 **small red pepper, finely chopped**	1/2 **teaspoon salt**
	1/8 **teaspoon turmeric**

In medium bowl, with fork, mash tofu until it resembles scrambled eggs; stir in celery, red pepper, green onion, mayonnaise, salt, and turmeric. Cover and refrigerate up to 1 day if not serving right away.

Each serving: About 195 calories, 18 g protein, 10 g carbohydrate, 11 g total fat (1 g saturated), 1 g fiber, 0 mg cholesterol, 455 mg sodium.

SERVING SUGGESTION
Whole-wheat pita breads with lettuce and tomatoes.

Index

A

Adobo, 110, 122
After-work chicken soup, 24
Alcohol, 9
Almonds, 46
Anchovies, 62, 72, 165
Apples:
    cider, 105
    Gala, 105
    Golden delicious, 105
    juice, 105
Apricot preserves, 108
Apricot-mustard glazed ham, 108
Artichokes, 82, 205
Arugula, 46, 51, 136, 143, 176
Arugula and watercress salad, 46
Arugula salad with citrus vinaigrette, 51
Asian fish sauce, 42, 67, 150, 210
Asian flounder bake, 180
Asian sesame oil, 21, 26, 66, 80, 85, 135, 175, 180, 209
Asparagus, 21, 23, 118, 125, 149, 193, 198, 201
Asparagus and endive salad with orange-mustard vinaigrette, 118
Asparagus and green-onion frittata, 198–199
Autumn tomato salsa, 72
Avocado, 99, 109, 122, 138, 213
Avocado-tomato salad, 99

B

Baby spinach and beet salad, 85
Bacon, 14, 60, 133, 159, 203
Barbecue sauce, 140
Basic fluffy omlet, 212
Bass, sea. See Sea bass.
BBQ pork chops, 131
Beans:
    green, 36, 90, 121, 162, 185
    roma, 143

Béarnaise sauce, 22
Beef, 59–99
    chuck, 60
    flank steak, 68, 84, 93, 94
    loin porterhouse, 72
    rib-eyes, 75, 86, 88, 91
    skirt steaks, 71, 99
    t-bone, 72
    tenderloin steaks, 63, 66, 87, 97
    top loin, 62, 75, 86
    top round steak, 67, 77, 80
    top sirloin, 80
Beef burgundy, 60
Beef tenderloins in marmalade pan sauce, 87
Beefsteak florentine with autumn tomato salsa, 72–73
Beer, 34
Beer can chicken, 34–35
Beets, 85
Benne. See Sesame seeds.
Benne biscuits, 191
Berries, 213
Black forest ham-wrapped asparagus, 193
Black-pepper beef roast with shallot sauce, 88
Blood sugar, 10
Bok choy, 167, 181
Bow-tie pasta, 24
Braised leeks, 174
Brandy, 97
Bread:
    challah, 40
    crumbs, 65, 136, 168
    French, 62
    whole-wheat toast, 213
Broccoli, 19, 66, 80, 93, 95, 171
Brussels sprouts, 47
Butterflied lamb with Moroccan flavors, 112
Buttermilk, 109, 191

C

Cabbage, 35, 42
  red, 35
  savoy, 159
Caesar salad, 165,
Cajun ham steak, 103
Cajun seasoniing, 103, 172
Cajun shrimp with rémoulade sauce,
  172–173
Calories, 9, 11
Canadian-style bacon, 194
Cantaloupe, 32
Capers, 52, 148, 155, 168, 184, 213
Caponata, 213
Carbohydrates, 9–12
  complex, 9–12
  simple, 9–12
Carrots, 14, 24, 35, 42, 50, 60, 61, 95,
  105, 132, 150, 167, 180, 210
Cauliflower, 74, 134
Celery, 14, 24, 36, 40, 47, 50, 51, 61,
  76, 147, 172, 200, 215
Cheese, 187–215
  Brie, 213
  Cheddar, 214
  feta, 68, 113, 142, 160, 183, 188,
    213
  goat, 205, 213
  Gruyère, 123, 193
  Montrachet, 205
  mozzarella, 25, 56, 211
  Neufchâtel, 198
  Parmesan, 56, 62, 65, 169, 176,
    193, 194, 206, 211, 213, 214
  Pecorino Romano, 143, 197
  Pepper Jack, 213
  ricotta, 206, 213
  ricotta salata, 142
  Romano, 136, 165
  Swiss, 123
Chicken, 13–57, 203
Chicken salad, 42
Chicken soup, 24
Chicken with pears and marsala, 18–19
Chile-rubbed ham with peach salsa, 122

Chiles:
  chipotle, 28, 99, 110, 122
  jalapeño, 31, 35, 36, 48, 102, 122,
    138, 156, 213
Chili powder, 44, 75, 112, 147
Chile steak with avocado-tomato
  salad, 99
Chilled buttermilk-vegetable soup, 109
Chimichurri sauce, 71
Chinese five-spice powder, 26, 156
Chinese five-spice grilled chicken,
  26–27
Cholesterol, 9
Chunky Greek salad, 113
Citrus fruit, 51
Citrus vinaigrette, 51
Clam juice, 147, 158
Coconut milk, 48, 210
Cod fillet, 159
Cod with cabbage, 159
Coffee, instant, 84
Coffee-and-spice steak with cool salsa,
  84
Collard greens, 130
Collards with pickled red onions, 130
Coq au vin, 14–15
Corn, 104
Corn and red pepper salsa, 104
Cream:
  half-and-half, 123
  heavy, 23, 97
  light, 123
  whipping, 23, 97
Cream cheese, 198, 213
Creamy asparagus soup, 23
Creamy mustard and dill sauce, 129
Crepes, French-style, 123
Cuban mojo pork chops, 110–111
Cucumber and cherry-tomato salad, 26
Cucumber and red onion salad, 56
Cucumber salad, 146
Cucumber raita, 126
Cucumbers, 26, 56, 135, 146
  English, 48, 84, 109, 160, 162,
    179, 183
  Kirby, 31, 113, 126, 155, 177, 183
Currants, 107

Curried chicken with mango and cataloupe slaw, 32–33
Curried pork medallions, 105
Curry powder, 32, 105

D

Dietary guidelines, 9
Diets, 11–12
Dill sauce, 129
Dilled tuna-stuffed tomatoes, 155

E

Egg salad deluxe, 200
Eggs, 162, 187–215
    whites, 191
Eggs florentine, 194–195
Eggplant, 142, 211
    Japanese, 102, 151
Endive, Belgian, 118, 210
Escarole, 92
Escarole with raisins and pignoli, 92
Exercise, 9

F

Fat, 9
    monounsaturated, 9
    polyunsaturated, 9
    saturated, 9
    trans, 9
Fajitas meat. *See* Beef, skirt steak.
Fennel :
    bulbs, 47, 61, 158
    seeds, 47, 63, 119, 126, 164
Fiber, 9–11
Fisherman's stew, 158
Flame-cooked chicken saltimbocca, 57
Flounder fillets, 157, 180
Flounder pesto roll-ups, 157
Food guide pyramid, 10
Frittatas, 188, 197, 198
Fruits, 9
    dried, 40

G

Garlic-crumbed tomatoes, 64–65

Garlicky spinach, 104
Ginger-jalapeño slaw, 35
Gingery Japanese eggplant, 151
Glazed salmon with watermelon salsa, 156
Glucose, 10
Glycemic index, 10–11
Grain, whole, 9
Grapefruit, 51, 210
Green beans. *See* beans.
Green beans with oven-roasted tomatoes, 90
Greens, baby, 122, 162, 194
Greens, salad, 57, 194
Grilled chicken with red-pepper salsa, 36–37
Grilled portobello mushroom salad, 176
Grilled steak caesar salad, 62
Grilled tofu and veggies, 202
Grilled tuna on spinach salad, 179
Gruyère and mushroom crepes, 123

H

Ham, 213
    Black Forest, 193
    deli, 43, 123
    shank, 108
    spiral-cut, 128
    steak, 103, 122
Herb and feta frittata, 188–189
Herbed yogurt sauce, 102
Herbes de Provence, 164
Hoisin glaze, 202
Hoisin sauce, 26, 93, 95, 135, 156, 202
Hominy, 138
Honey, 28, 43, 78, 99, 128
Honey glaze, 28
Honey-glazed spiral-cut ham, 128
Horseradish, white, 89
Horseradish cream, 89
Hot and sour soup, 209

J

Japanese bread crumbs. See Panko.
Jerk pork chops with grilled pineapple, 114–115

Jerk seasoning, 114

K

Kale, 35
Kansas City Ribs, 140–141
Ketchup, 172
Korean-style sirloin, 80–81

L

Lamb, 101–143
    ground, 102
    leg, 112, 126
    leg steaks, 107
Lamb and vegetable kabobs, 102
Leeks, 24, 174
Lemon broccoli, 170–171
Lemon dressing, 61
Lemon-fennel roasted chicken pieces,
    47
Lemon-marinated mushrooms, 53
Lemons, 22, 36, 47, 52, 54, 61, 82,
    129, 153, 158, 164, 168, 171, 172
    juice, 36, 53, 57, 62, 102, 113,
        126, 136, 148, 155, 160, 165,
        172, 177
    peel, 17, 86, 168, 172, 208
Lemony veal and baby artichokes,
    82–83
Lettuce, 215
    Boston, 32, 61, 162, 200
    romaine, 62, 165
Lighter beef and broccoli, 66
Limes, 16, 32, 43, 78, 84, 103, 109,
    114, 149, 156
    juice, 28, 42, 99, 104, 110, 122,
        146, 150, 179, 210
    peel, 86, 179
London broil with garlic and herbs, 77

M

Mandarin oranges, 203
Mango, 32, 213
Mango chutney, 213
Mango and cantaloupe slaw, 32–33
Maple-glazed pork tenderloins, 133

Maple syrup, 133
Marinara sauce, 56, 131
Marinated flank steak with grilled
    summer squash, mushroom and feta
    "lasagna", 68–69
Mayonnaise, 129, 155, 165, 169, 172,
    215
Mediterranean grilled eggplant and
    summer squash, 142
Mediterranean grilled sea bass, 152–
    153
Mediterranean swordfish salad, 160–
    161
Mesclun salad greens, 169
Mesclun salad with parmesan polenta
    rounds, 169
Middle Eastern lamb steaks, 106–107
Milk, 129, 188, 190, 194, 198, 206,
    214
    buttermilk, 109, 191
Minerals, 9–10
Mixed pea pod stir-fry, 185
Mixed summer squash with parsley
    and lemon, 208
Molasses, 131
Monkfish, 158
Mushrooms, 14, 53, 60, 95, 98, 200,
    214
    cremini, 123
    oyster, 98
    portobello, 68, 71, 102, 176
    shiitake, 98, 209, 214
Mussels, 158, 184
Mussels with capers and white wine,
    184
Mustard:
    Dijon, 20, 28, 43, 46, 51, 108, 118,
        128, 129, 142, 155, 162, 165,
        169, 172, 203
    dry, 62
    seeds, 121, 126

N

Nectarine salad with prosciutto,
78–79
Nectarines, 78, 177
North African flank steak, 94

Nutritional content, 11

O

Okra, 76
Okra with tomatoes, 76
Olives, 36
   green, 164
   kalamata, 113
   niçoise, 162
Omelet, 212
Onions, 14, 17, 23, 38, 40, 42, 44, 50,
   60, 76, 87, 110, 131, 138, 140,
   147, 158, 197, 200
   green, 23, 28, 29, 35, 84, 102, 104,
      113, 117, 135, 147, 150, 156,
      167, 172, 175, 177, 180, 198,
      202, 209, 210, 213, 214, 215
   red, 36, 56, 67, 75, 102, 107, 130,
      136, 164, 183, 213
   spring, 197
Orange and sage roasted turkey and
   gravy, 38–39, 41
Orange marmalade, 87
Orange pork and asparagus stir-fry,
   124–125
Oranges, 38, 44, 110, 111, 118, 140
   mandarine, 203
   navel, 118, 125
   peel, 164
Oven-roasted tomatoes, 90

P

Pan-fried steaks with spinach and
   tomatoes, 86
Panko, 20
Panko-mustard chicken, 20
Parsley vinaigrette, 162
Peaches, 28, 43, 122
   jam or preserves, 122
   salsa, 28, 122
Peanut butter, 48
Peanuts, 42, 146
Pears, 19
Peas, 185
Pepper-crusted filet mignon, 63
Pepperoncini, 36

Peppers, 63
   green, 76, 102
   red, 68, 74, 75, 93, 102, 104, 113,
      117, 147, 202, 210, 215
   hot, 28
   roasted, 36, 138
   yellow, 51, 95
Pesto, 157, 213
Philadelphia steak. See Beef, skirt
   steak.
Phyllo, 205
Pickled green beans, 121
Pignoli. See Pine nuts.
Pine nuts, 92, 107
Pineapple, 114
Pistachios, 78
Pita bread, 159, 197, 203, 215
Poached chicken piccata, 52
Polenta, precooked, 169, 194
Pork, 101–143
   baby back ribs, 140
   chops, 110, 114, 117, 136
   loin, 119, 131
   shoulder blade roast, 138
   tenderloin, 105, 125, 133, 135
Pork and posole stew, 138–139
Pork chops with peppers and onions,
   116–117
Pork chops with tomato and arugula,
   136–137
Portion control, 11
Posole, 138
Potatoes, red, 162
Poultry, 13–57
Prosciutto, 57, 78, 193
Protein, 9
Provençal salmon, 164
Pyramid, food. See Food guide
   pyramid.

R

Radishes, 61, 67, 138, 179
Raisins, golden, 44, 51, 92
Red pepper vinaigrette, 75
Red peppers. See Peppers.
Red snapper, 150
Red-pepper salsa, 36

Rémoulade sauce, 172
Ribs, 140
Rice, brown, 19, 135, 147
Roast chicken béarnaise, 22
Roast salmon with capers and
    tarragon, 168, 170
Roasted asparagus, 201
Roasted cauliflower, 134
Roasted cauliflower with red pepper, 74
Roasted eggplant parmesan, 211
Roasted prosciutto-wrapped asparagus,
    192–193

S
Salad greens, 57, 194
Salad niçoise, 162–163
Salami:
    genoa, 143
    sopressata, 143
Salmon, 156, 164, 168, 175, 177, 179
    smoked, 213
Salmon steaks with nectarine salad,
    177
Salmon teriyaki, 175
Salmon with tomato-olive relish, 164
Salsa, 84, 213
Salt, 9
Saltimbocca, chicken, 57
Sausage:
    Hot Italian, 197
    pork, 40
    sweet Italian, 197
Sausage and herb bread stuffing,
    40
Sautéed mixed mushrooms, 98
Scrambled eggs with chives, 190
Scrod, 167
Sea bass, 153
Seafood, 145–185
Sesame-aparagus stir-fry, 21
Sesame pork tenderloins, 135
Sesame seeds, 26, 85, 135, 180, 191
Shallots, 20, 22, 48, 53, 72, 82, 88, 91,
    98, 118, 176, 184
Sherry, dry, 26, 93, 180
Shredded carrots, 132
Shrimp, 146, 147, 158, 172, 183

Shrimp and tomato summer salad,
    182–183
Shrimp Étouffée, 147
Shrimp saté with cucumber salad, 146
Skate, 148
Skate with brown butter, lemon, and
    capers, 148
Skillet asparagus, 149
Skillet cherry tomatoes, 212
Skillet chicken parmesan, 56
Skirt steak with chimichurri sauce,
    70–71
Snapper, 150
Snow peas, 185
Sole fillets, 180
Sopressata and roma bean salad with
    pecorino, 143
Sour cream, 89, 129, 213
Soy sauce, 21, 26, 48, 66, 68, 80, 85,
    93, 167, 180, 181, 185, 202, 209
Spice-brined pork loin, 119–120
Spiced grilled turkey breast, 28–30
Spiced lamb, 126
Spicy garlic lamb with cucumber
    raita, 126–127
Spicy ground lamb and vegetable
    kabobs with herbed yogurt sauce,
    102–103
Spinach, 85, 86, 104, 111, 179, 180,
    194, 197, 203, 214
Spinach roulade with mushrooms, 214
Spinach salad, 179
Spinach salad with oranges, 111
Spinach salad with warm bacon
    dressing, 203
Spring onion, spinach and Pecorino
    frittata, 196–197
Squash, summer, 17, 54, 68, 107, 142,
    208
Steak au poivre, 96–97
Steak with shallot-red wine sauce, 91
Steamed scrod fillets, 166–167
Stir-fried bok choy, 181
Stir-fry, 93, 95, 181
Strip steak with red pepper vinaigrette,
    75
Sugar, 9
Sugar snap peas, 185

Summer squash and chicken, 54–55
Summer squash with herbs, 17
Swordfish steak, 160

T

Tangerine beef stir-fry, 93
Tangerines, 93
Teriyaki sauce, 151, 175
Thai beef salad, 67
Thai chicken saté, 48–49
Thai coconut soup, 210
Thai green curry paste, 48
Thai snapper, 150
Tofu, 202, 209, 210, 215
Tofu "Egg-salad", 215
Tomato and cheese pie, 206–207
Tomato-olive relish, 164
Tomato, smoked chicken, and
    mozzarella salad, 25
Tomato jam, 44
Tomato paste, 14, 60, 147
Tomato sauce, 140
Tomatoes, 25, 65, 76, 107, 109, 136,
    138, 155, 158, 162, 164, 183, 206,
    213, 215
    cherry, 26, 86, 99, 160, 205, 212,
        214
    grape, 86, 113, 160, 205
    oven-roasted, 90
    plum, 44, 56, 72, 75, 90, 157, 211
Tortillas, 135
Tossed salad, 57, 123
Tuna, 155, 162, 179
Tuna with spice rub, 179
Turkey, 14–57
    brined, 28
    smoked, 213
Turkey breast with roasted vegetable
    gravy, 50–51
Turkey cutlets, Indian style, 16
Turkey kabobs with garden tomato
    jam, 44–45

U

U.S. Department of Agriculture, 9, 10

V

Veal, 82
Vegetable gravy, 50
Vegetable salad with fresh lemon
    dressing, 61
Vegetable stir-fry, 95
Vegetables, 9, 187–215
Vegetarian phyllo pizza, 204–205
Vietnamese-style chicken salad, 42–43
Vinegar:
    balsamic, 28, 68, 72, 87, 169, 176
    cider, 51, 140, 203
    red wine, 25, 31, 46, 71, 75, 77,
        130, 131, 142, 162, 183
    rice, 35, 48, 85, 118, 151, 167,
        202, 209
    sherry, 46
    tarragon, 22
    white, 121
    white wine, 22, 169
Vitamins, 9–11

W

Watercress, 43, 46, 67, 78, 210
Watercress and peach salad with
    turkey, 43
Watermelon, 31, 84, 156
Watermelon salad, 31
Wine:
    marsala, 19
    red, 14, 60, 91
    white, 22, 97, 158, 157, 184
Worcestershire sauce, 62, 165, 209

Y

Yogurt, 16, 32, 102, 126

Z

Zucchini, 17, 54, 68, 107, 142, 154,
    202, 208
Zucchini ribbons with mint, 154

Metric Equivalents

The recipes that appear in this cookbook use the standard United States method for measuring liquid and dry or solid ingredients (teaspoons, tablespoons, and cups). The information on this chart is provided to help cooks outside the U.S. successfully use these recipes. All equivalents are approximate.

METRIC EQUIVALENTS FOR DIFFERENT TYPES OF INGREDIENTS

A standard cup measure of a dry or solid ingredient will vary in weight depending on the type of ingredient. A standard cup of liquid is the same volume for any type of liquid. Use the following chart when converting standard cup measures to grams (weight) or milliliters (volume).

Standard Cup	Fine Powder (e.g. flour)	Grain (e.g. rice)	Granular (e.g. sugar)	Liquid Solids (e.g. butter)	Liquid (e.g. milk)
1	140 g	150 g	190 g	200 g	240 ml
$3/4$	105 g	113 g	143 g	150 g	180 ml
$2/3$	93 g	100 g	125 g	133 g	160 ml
$1/2$	70 g	75 g	95 g	100 g	120 ml
$1/3$	47 g	50 g	63 g	67 g	80 ml
$1/4$	35 g	38 g	48 g	50 g	60 ml
$1/8$	18 g	19 g	24 g	25 g	30 ml

USEFUL EQUIVALENTS FOR LIQUID INGREDIENTS BY VOLUME

$1/4$ tsp =					1 ml
$1/2$ tsp =					2 ml
1 tsp =					5 ml
3 tsp =	1 tbls =		$1/2$ fl oz	=	15 ml
	2 tbls =	$1/8$ cup =	1 fl oz	=	30 ml
	4 tbls =	$1/4$ cup =	2 fl oz	=	60 ml
	$5 1/3$ tbls =	$1/3$ cup =	3 fl oz	=	80 ml
	8 tbls =	$1/2$ cup =	4 fl oz	=	120 ml
	$10 2/3$ tbls =	$2/3$ cup =	5 fl oz	=	160 ml
	12 tbls =	$3/4$ cup =	6 fl oz	=	180 ml
	16 tbls =	1 cup =	8 fl oz	=	240 ml
	1 pt =	2 cups =	16 fl oz	=	480 ml
	1 qt =	4 cups =	32 fl oz	=	960 ml
			33 fl oz	= 1000 ml	= 1 l

USEFUL EQUIVALENTS FOR DRY INGREDIENTS BY WEIGHT

(To convert ounces to grams, multiply the number of ounces by 30.)

1 oz	=	$1/16$ lb	=	30 g
4 oz	=	$1/4$ lb	=	120 g
8 oz	=	$1/2$ lb	=	240 g
12 oz	=	$3/4$ lb	=	360 g
16 oz	=	1 lb	=	480 g

USEFUL EQUIVALENTS FOR COOKING/OVEN TEMPERATURES

	Fahrenheit	Celsius	Gas Mark
Freeze Water	32° F	0° C	
Room Temperature	68° F	20° C	
Boil Water	212° F	100° C	
Bake	325° F	160° C	3
	350° F	180° C	4
	375° F	190° C	5
	400° F	200° C	6
	425° F	220° C	7
	450° F	230° C	8
Broil			Grill

USEFUL EQUIVALENTS FOR LENGTH

(To convert inches to centimeters, multiply the number of inches by 2.5.)

1 in	=		2.5 cm
6 in	=	$1/2$ ft =	15 cm
12 in	=	1 ft =	30 cm
36 in	=	3 ft = 1 yd =	90 cm
40 in	=		100 cm = 1 m